Woman Reinvented

Reweaving the fabric of your life after divorce

Cyndy Whitlock

R^ethink

First published in Great Britain in 2021 by Rethink Press
(www.rethinkpress.com)

Contents

Introduction

In 2019, after decades of trying to work through the seemingly endless challenges of being a married person, I finally threw in the towel. After forty-two years, I decided enough was enough.

I had lost all faith in what I had once believed in with all my heart. I had used up every resource I had trying to rekindle happiness in my home. My toolbox was empty. I simply had nothing left to give. I was worn down and played out. I had worked for decades to hold up my side of a bargain into which I had entered as a young woman, but, despite my best efforts, I alone could not patch up the rotting remnants of a life or repair the damage done. The entire fabric of the life I had worked so hard to preserve finally ripped right down the middle.

As I reflect on all of the laughter, tears, fears, gains and losses I had experienced over the years, I realized that for me the material that had bound me to the covenant I had entered so many years before had become a thread-bare palette of dull grays. No recognizable pattern was left – only a sad amalgam of faded brilliance pooled at the base of a mountain of pain. My disintegrating worldview meant that by the time I divorced, I could no longer see color at home, or at work, or in the light in my grandchildren's eyes.

Adrift

I am adrift in a sea of gray.
There is no color in my desolate domain.
A world where sounds shrink away and
A somber fog muffles the footsteps of all who
    enter and retreat.
There is no glow of light nor star-filled dark,
Only murky shadows that snuff out joy and
    remind me
How time and space have slipped away and
Dusk looms with every movement of the clock.
I am adrift in a sea of gray.
    – Cyndy Whitlock, 2018

The "why"

When I wrote that dark poem, I did not believe there was hope for my future. I thought I was too old, too wrung out, too used up. Although I longed for a return to a world filled with color and sunlight, deep down I held a grim belief that there was no way to reconstruct a life out of the ruin of my present state. I could not imagine how I would ever emerge from my personal abyss.

Although it took me another year and a half after I wrote "Adrift" to leave my marriage, I noticed that just by allowing myself to imagine a different life, I was occasionally seeing glimpses of color again. These infrequent glimpses held elusive promise, yet I continued to thrash about beneath the waves of my private losses, my disintegrating self-esteem and my crumbling belief in the life I had worked so hard to build.

I had become invisible. After the passage of many years and a long history of painful experiences, I was no longer a participant in my own life. I was repeatedly stunned and emotionally paralyzed by the cruel tricks life can play, dashing hopes and best laid plans. I felt like a cliché: aging woman disintegrates into shadowy irrelevance. I was aware of a vague sense of abandonment, of being left alone to fend for myself as I helplessly watched the demise of my marriage dream. I knew in my bones that something had long ago killed what had once been an overpowering love.

For years before I finally faced the truth, I tried to avoid looking at the problems. I was afraid to uncover what I already suspected to be true. To peek beneath the surface of who I had become and the relationship that defined my life was a frightening undertaking. Deep inside, I knew there were no more solutions left to try and nothing left to control or cure. Each moment of conflict, sudden anger or silent disdain drove home the truth about the next steps I would have to take. Ultimately, something unraveled and then finally shredded to tatters inside me.

Long ago, I learned that when I get in a dark emotional trench, I must reach out for help. I have never been able to confide in my family of origin, but the counsel of strangers has been supportive to me throughout my life. Joining two support groups during the final acts of the melodrama of my marriage gave me glimpses of hope. It was like feeling my way along the wall of a pitch-black and derelict coal mine, occasionally seeing a sliver of light ahead to hint that I might again one day stand on my own two feet in fresh air and the sunlight of the spirit.

Telling other people about my real life was agonizing at first. I have always been the calm, supportive presence in the lives of other people. I am the listener, not the speaker. I am the helper, not the one needing help. While these elements of my self-image are true, my healing has always been dependent on coming to terms with my own reality. Many times, I have reassured others that storytelling is a powerful way to heal old wounds, and as I have come through my late-in-life divorce and rewoven the fabric of my life, I have healed my perception of past wrongs by speaking my truth, telling my story.

Along with speaking my truth, writing has been one of my favorite tools for patching up my timeworn views about the past. When there was no one around in whom I could confide, my journal listened and never told my secrets to the world; so, when the facilitator of one of my support groups suggested I write a book about my healing process, I resisted at first, then nervously accepted the challenge.

As I began to write this book, I saw that after summing up my attempts to maintain the outside image of a happy home and improve life for everyone in my family, all my efforts had come down to one defining instant – my personal moment of reckoning. Years before this moment arrived, I realized that the gap between what I had hoped for and what I saw happening each day was widening, and there seemed to be nothing I could do to stop it. As my ability to honestly communicate my feelings broke down, the distance grew between how I wanted things to be and my awareness of how things were.

In a desperate effort to preserve my own sanity, I went alone to a therapist who was familiar with problems in family dynamics. He worked with me to help me clean up my side of the street. He made it clear that the purpose of our work together was not to save my marriage or change my spouse. My solo work was to focus only on the problems I brought to the table as well as my own unmet needs. Ultimately, I learned that my happiness was up to me and I was the only one who could change my circumstance. At the end of one of our sessions, he walked me to the door of his office and calmly said, "You know, Cyndy, nothing changes if nothing changes."

I drove home in tears, and when I got there, I walked wordlessly into the house. I stood frozen just inside the door, feet glued to the floor, my purse still hanging from my shoulder. On the opposite wall were photographs of what appeared to be a normal life. This room should have been warm and familiar to me. I had decorated it, for heaven's sake! But at that moment I could have been standing on the cold tundra of the Arctic. I knew I was about to witness a fatality, the death of something I had believed in my whole adult life. Clarity was staring me in the face, and I knew there was nothing more I could do but turn and face the wind.

This was the moment when I felt the permanent rip in my fabric. I knew the support structure I had worked so hard to preserve had suffered irreparable damage. Although I had always treasured loyalty above all other values, I knew right then and there that I had to choose between, on the one hand, betraying a deeply held core value and, on the other hand, staying in that house, that marriage, and accepting that this was all I was and all I would ever be. Choosing to stay would require me to accept the death of my own soul.

While deep rips in the fabric of one's life are permanent and painful, they do not have to be fatal to the mind, body, or spirit. However, to surrender a long-held guiding principle for the sake of an unknown future is a scary proposition. To release that which no longer serves us, placing our trust in the Divine Knowing to show us where and with whom our souls can be fulfilled, is an easy thing to do while sitting quietly in meditation on a yoga mat. However, it is a daunting endeavor when we step off the mat to face the stark realities of the real world.

When I started this journey, I had no way of knowing that by releasing attachments to old thought patterns, beliefs and behaviors, I would make space for providence to step in. While I had been preoccupied with surrendering my future to the dominion of gray, the Divine Knowing was designing a return to vivid color that I could not have imagined for myself. The universe was planning a big reveal party, but I first had to get out of her way.

On a warm August evening, I was sitting in our bedroom, contemplating leaving and making a mental list of things I should take with me. I gazed around the room, noting the golden wall color I had chosen, the matching comforter on the bed, the pieces of artwork that adorned the walls. In this room, I had created what I hoped would be a sanctuary of peace, but the juxtaposition of that image and the reality I had lived suddenly struck me right between the eyes. This so-called sanctuary held no peace, no sense of comfort. It had become a place of emptiness from which I only wanted to escape.

As I sat there, stuck in the inertia of my own inaction, I began to ask myself what I was waiting for. Through my counseling, I had learned where my limits were and how much I was capable of. What was stopping me now? My mind and heart flooded with motivation and I immediately set to packing as if the house were on fire. My heart was pounding in my chest, empowering me to take the action I had dreaded for so long. I threw my things into boxes with abandon and was out of the house by that evening.

Of course, I had nowhere to go, and as I drove away I laughed a little at my impulsive decision to leave that night. My life had never followed a neat pattern of moving directly from point A to B to C, and here I was, bumbling through yet another badly timed episode. The thought of starting anything over at my age seemed ridiculous. How could I ever recover financially? How would I ever find another love in my life, or even a companion? I had never lived alone – how would I manage that?

I didn't have answers for any of these questions, yet I was convinced that staying in my marital home was no longer an option. Despite feeling scared and dejected, I kept my foot on the gas pedal and drove off into the dark. That night I moved into a long-term utility hotel and although I didn't realize it at the time, from that austere little room I began the journey of reinvention I am still on today. I did not grasp that I had turned a page in my life that, for better or worse, could not be unturned. I had stepped through the rip in my fabric, a passage into a whole new life that would lead me to new people, new places, new work, new experiences and dazzling new colors.

Slowly, I began to see that I had been given an opportunity to stitch the rest of my life into whatever color and texture I wanted. Perhaps I would travel, or write, or renew my career. I began to fantasize about a whole host of things I might do with the rest of my life. I saw the remaining time I had as a precious gift I did not want to waste. How many years I had left was unknown, but I decided to use whatever time I did have fully engaged with the business and pleasure of living.

I resolved to design a new fabric for my future, a garment that would be handmade by me and for me. If I were to never again be loved by another person, I would get better at loving myself. I would defeat the old patterns I had lived with for so long. I would handpick the threads I would use to weave a new tapestry from healthier decisions and colorful achievements. I knew that my decision to leave would cost me dearly. I would lose many of my friends, my home, my town and my moorings, but I was determined to learn to finally value myself and the daughter, sister, wife, mother, colleague and friend I had been to so many for so long.

I began to write every day about my experiences, and, as I wrote, I developed a handbook for reinventing myself – a map to show me how to reconnect with color and revitalize my life through reinvestment in my bliss. I began to recognize that the tools I was developing for myself as I moved along my pathway to healing might assist others whose life fabrics had likewise been torn. I was creating the life plan I had long searched for, a blueprint for living that would lead me to realization, redefinition, rediscovery, and reinvention.

I want to be clear: I am not a therapist. I am just a person whose life plan had to change at a late stage, and a woman who has cut a trail through an unexpected wilderness. I do not see myself as a guru, but I do know the pain of having your life flipped on its ear, and I know that curling up into a ball and giving away what is left of your personal power is not the answer.

Life crises test our mettle and give us opportunities and motivations to rise like the phoenix to try again. Reinvention is the quintessence of a life lived beyond the edges of survival. All women have a phoenix within, a goddess energy that embodies the creation of life. People who live meaningful lives periodically reinvent themselves. They view the bumps in the road not as failures, but as indicators that a change of course is necessary. As much as we may feel stuck, we have no choice but to engage with the life force within. We are either moving forward or falling behind; nothing exists in-between.

The "how"

If you are facing a rip in the fabric of your own life, I offer you the following chapters, which outline the steps I took to reinvent my life and change my world from gray to living color. Each chapter represents a thread in the new fabric of my life. As you move through the chapters, you can try on new garments of reinvention for yourself.

When I started my journey of reinvention, I rejected shades of gray and instead stitched a fresh bolt of cloth, woven with vibrantly colored threads. I researched the meanings of colors in cultures from all over the world, and I created the Reinvention Color Association Chart (RCAC) to help me determine my own personal colors of reinvention. Naturally, your personal colors will be exactly that – your own. As you will see when you engage with the RCAC, color association is a highly personal endeavor that no single philosophy or practice can dictate.

The same is true for talisman selection. You will note as you read this book that each chapter describes an object, a charm of sorts, that I used to encourage me on my steps of self-discovery. Although a talisman is not a necessary part of reinvention, I found the search for a talisman a poignant reminder that, just as I already owned possessions that had soothed or healed me over time, I likewise already possessed the emotional and intellectual wherewithal to reinvent myself from the inside out.

The RCAC and a guide for selecting a talisman, as well as guide sheets for the journaling stems found at the end of each chapter, are available for free on my coaching and teaching website: www.reinventioninprogress .com. There you can also join an online community or register for a course that will provide additional guidance for digesting the content of this book.

None of us have a crystal ball, but we all possess the power to redefine our experience, to reimagine what could be, and to reinvent the kind of life we want to be living now. If you are living in the aftermath of a broken relationship, this book is for you.

The "who"

You are "the who." I designed the following chapters to help you reinvent yourself. No single event should ever be allowed to define who we are for the rest of our lives. You were not born to satisfy someone else's expectations, and none of us can afford to rest on the glories or the catastrophes of our pasts. There is nothing to be gained by sitting around waiting for this amazing life expedition to end. Miscalculations and mistakes are gifts from the universe to be used as guideposts for navigation. Buy yourself a beautiful journal in which to document your steps. Get up, stay strong, and steel your own determination to "walk out to walk on" (Wheatley and Frieze, 2011).

A couple of years ago, a friend told me that "with a fair wind," I might have another thirty or forty years left to live. She strongly suggested that it was up to me what to make of those years. I cautiously wondered if I could create a whole new life in the time I had left.

I finally decided to take my friend's words to heart and have never looked back. I was inspired by the optimism they imbued and intrigued by the colorful pictures that began to develop in my mind. I could rise again. I could sketch a new pattern. I could make a new garment that would reflect the complex and delightful concoction that is me. Those words foretold the reinvented woman I am today.

I invite you to read this book, write your plan and join me on this adventurous heart journey. A bright and color-washed world is open for all of us. Reinvention awaits just around the corner and, "with a fair wind," we will all get there together.

ONE
Remembering:
The Purple Thread

While going through my divorce, memories rushed in on me so fast, I often felt like I was being swept over the edge of a great waterfall. I experienced frequent moments of anxiety and disbelief. "Is this really happening – I mean to me, here, now, at this late hour of my life?" For the first few months after I left, I awoke on many mornings with an initial sense of relief, thinking, "Oh, that was just a dream," only to be slammed in the face with the sudden realization that, "Nope, this is your new reality. No more marriage, no more home, no more security."

The good news was that the further time took me from my marital home, the more color began to seep back into my conscious thoughts. But I wanted more than seepage: I desired to once again experience the sensual connection to color I had enjoyed in my youth. As a younger woman, I had loved sewing fine fabrics, wearing bright clothes and making imaginative pottery. I wanted color to once again be a driving force that would lead me away from gray thoughts and gray actions. I sought to taste color, see color, touch color. I wanted to smell the richness of the hues around me and wrap myself in the warm blanket of my life.

Color associations are not universal. They are deeply private and often subconscious choices we all make based on how we perceive our possessions and the events of our lives. Culture affects our reactions to color, as do our good or bad memories that we associate with certain tints and tones. As you examine the Reinvention Color Association Chart, you will choose the color of each thread you will weave into the reinvented fabric of your life. You may also choose to identify an object, a talisman you already possess that represents the reasoning behind your color choices.

As I considered colors and the pictures they painted in my mind, I decided that my prevailing tint for "remembering" was purple. For me, purple is a pigment of low light and low arousal. It was the perfect color to apply during my first forays into healing because I knew it would soothe me as I explored the mysteries of how and why I had fallen so low. For some, purple is a regal color, but for me, it opens my mind to nostalgia and sentiment but does not bring on depression. Purple stimulates my memory and reinforces my spiritual connections. When I settle into purple, I feel safe in its jewel-toned embrace. I can look at my marital past in an unvarnished way. Purple allows me to face the truth about other people and myself – my strengths and deficits, as well as my personalized process of reinvention.

As I gave thought to finding a purple talisman, I remembered a chunk of violet amethyst I have had for years. It is a lovely sample of quartz cluster crystal, which is thought by some practitioners of natural healing to be a stone that cleanses negative energy and reduces anxiety (Nall, 2020). Although there is no scientific evidence to support this claim, I think of amethyst as an absorbing substance that clears my thinking and helps me to balance the physical, mental and spiritual parts of me.

Given the lack of scientific support for any healing claims regarding crystals in general, I do not place much stock in amethyst's power to heal my pain, but I do know that when I meditate on purple, I feel less stressed and more able to embrace my journey of reinvention and face the candid truth about my past.

My marriage story

Looking back now, I am amused when I think of how carefully I tried to chart each step of my life, only to receive a monumental curve ball forty years later. I certainly never included an eventual divorce as part of my life plan.

I married in 1977 when I was just twenty years old. I can grin today at my sheltered young self who believed she had the knowledge and understanding to select a mate for life. I was as certain as one could be that I had found my one true love, my soul mate. I was raised to believe in such fairy tales and looking back on my wedding day I had no doubt that I would remain beside my new spouse forever, through thick and thin, sickness and health, ups and downs – through anything and everything life could or would ever throw at us.

I suppose most couples feel something similar when they stand together and commit their lives to one another, but as I reflect on that day, knowing what I know now, I see a young girl who really was in love with being in love. I wanted to believe that someone could passionately love me forever. I desired a man who would be my rock, my unchanging stability, my protector from all that was wrong in the world. But sadly, I was clueless about how marriage was supposed to work, ignorant about how healthy people solve problems, and totally naïve when it came to handling tough times and communicating my own needs.

Knowing what both of my parents already knew about the struggles of life, I am surprised that neither of them tried to talk me out of getting married at such a young age. After all, their life together had not been all sweetness and solidarity. At times, my father could be a funny man, pulling pranks on kids and tapping into a boyish charm when talking with neighbors and the customers he served. But behind closed doors, he was frequently intractable, routinely moody and often morose. My mother was physically unwell much of the time and struggled to hang on when Dad's emotional rollercoaster was set roaring on its track.

By the time my wedding rolled around, my older sister was already married and gone from the house. My father had repeatedly told us both that once we were out of his home, that was it: no more free rides. There was no going back, no undoing an ill-advised youthful choice, no redeeming a losing proposition. No matter what had eventually taken me out of his house, once gone I could never live there again. I know he loved us, but he believed he had done his part when we were kids, and once we were emancipated it was our responsibility to take it from there.

I think my dad believed my marriage set him free from a twenty-year sentence with a ball and chain. At our wedding reception, he announced that he had done his duty and henceforth I was no longer his "problem." Though I felt a pang of injury when I heard him say that, I did not realize the full weight of the message my father conveyed that day. Embedded in his words was the implication that wives create problems, women need to be dominated, and it was now up to someone else to tame the wildness I embodied.

That public announcement, painful as it was, was not in itself the saddest part of that memory for me. The most heartbreaking aspect of this exchange was that I was standing right there. Dad's comments were not hidden from me or said behind my back. They were overt and out loud, but – because of my upbringing and societal indoctrination about the role of women – I accepted his misogynistic message that I was a problematic piece of property. Like an unruly horse, my will had to be broken to maintain patriarchal control and allow peace to reign in any environment into which I would enter.

I often wondered over the course of what I considered to be a bumpy married life why my mother never encouraged me to slow down, to take the time to really know whomever I might marry, to pause before committing my life to any man. Sadly, my mother died when I was twenty-five, but if I could speak to her today I would ask her why she never encouraged me to give such a momentous decision more time for deeper deliberation.

As a headstrong young woman, I was hellbent on getting married, and there was probably nothing my mother or father could have said to deter me from my chosen path, but a sobering and honest conversation about the realities of married life never took place.

Had my parents and I been willing and able to speak openly about the possible pitfalls of marriage, I might have side-stepped years of heartaches.

Although I believed my youthful judgement was sound, I did not harbor a delusion that all marriages were flawless. I had seen too many arguments between my parents, too many days of silent disdain, to believe they were always happy together. Yet, somehow, I trusted that my marriage would be different – fueled only by undying love and mutual support. I had absolute faith that the love I had found was steadfast and unbreakable. Little did I know that my childlike faith was headed for a relentless confrontation with reality.

I've often wondered what my mom was thinking as I approached my big day with such confidence and self-importance. Perhaps my mother thought I would be better off living somewhere else, free of the dark clouds of smoldering anger that periodically descended over our house and hovered there until my dad decided it was alright for the sun to shine again. Perhaps she was living vicariously through me, imagining a new start with a young man who might not create as much daily drama as Dad did. Maybe she was simply afraid that her smart but socially awkward daughter would never find anyone else willing to marry her.

Whatever her reasons, she never tried to encourage me to date other people, travel, work or live on my own before marrying. She often spoke of how much she loved the man I chose. I believe she genuinely thought of him as the son she never had, and she welcomed him into her heart with open arms.

Many people who stay in long or lifetime marriages are relatively happy for many years. I suppose when most couples finally reach the 40 years of marriage mark, they speak of that accomplishment with a sense of pride. I always dreaded being asked how long I had been married because I anticipated the question that came next: "How'd you do it?"

The truth was, I had no idea. At ten years, sixteen years, twenty-five years, I knew my answers were starting to sound hollow, but I could still manage to reply with something jaunty and upbeat. As time continued to slip by, I could think of fewer and fewer positive responses; yet, with the passage of time, the expectations for an inspirational reply grew exponentially.

By the time I realized that forty-two years of my life had gone by, I had lost my sense of humor about marriage and I was fresh out of cheerful answers to the question of how I had managed to stay married for so long.

Attitudes and belief systems

The attitudes about relationships that our families of origin express often influence how we approach our marriages. Both of my parents came from what they referred to as "broken" homes – a term used frequently in the discourse of the twentieth century, particularly when describing reasons for a child's misbehavior, emotional difficulties or criminal acts. Divorce carried a significant social stigma, and my parents were both ashamed of their own parents' decisions to divorce. They also strongly linked deprivation and economic instability in their childhoods to the fact that their parents were not willing or able to hold things together, even for the sake of the children.

As a child, it was firmly impressed upon me that although there was discord in my home, the alternative of not having my parents together and living under the same roof was unthinkable. OK, so they had dark periods. I just chalked that up to being a normal part of how married people lived together. How was I to know that well-adjusted partners talk out their problems and find joint solutions?

That is not to say there were never any good moments in our home, and those good times also became part of my expectations for married life. But growing up I never trusted that good moments would last. Waiting around the corner was either a legitimate obstacle to be tackled or a problem of unknown origin that would infect us all until my dad decided the trouble was over. My mom humored him in his moodiness, and I suppose I learned that strategy from her. My parents were both good people and they did the best they could, but neither of them had the benefit of good role models for marriage.

I am sometimes in awe that my parents were able to keep things stable, even some of the time. Because of the circumstances life handed them, both my mom and dad developed sturdy work ethics and a never-say-die attitude about life, and I think that kept them persevering in their shared existence. Both of my parents were children of the Great Depression and members of the so-called Greatest Generation. They repeatedly told us that love was work, marriage was work, raising kids was work, work was work – everything was work. If you did not work, you were considered a lazy malingerer.

These beliefs were burned into my psyche at an early age and undoubtedly contributed to my die-hard attitude about my own marriage. I certainly believed that I needed to work at my marriage and stay with it to the bitter end. Had I been born into an earlier generation, I would have likely stayed married for life, no matter what. However, I was born during a time of great social and political change, and, like every generation, the divorce data for Baby Boomers reflects the conditions of our times.

In her 2017 article titled "Led by Baby Boomers, divorce rates climb for America's 50+ population,"

Renee Stepler wrote for the Pew Research Center that "so-called 'gray divorce' is on the rise." Using statistics gathered from the National Center of Health Statistics and the US Census Bureau, Stepler concluded that "among those ages 65 and older, the divorce rate has roughly tripled since 1990." Perhaps I was not as alone in my divorce experience as I felt. I was indeed living through a "gray divorce."

Over the course of my Baby Boomer life, divorce lost much of its stigma, more women carved out careers and earning power for themselves, and cohabitation without marriage became more socially acceptable. Divorce does not raise eyebrows anymore, and the growing divorce rate for people over the age of sixty reflects that trend.

In a survey conducted in 2013 by the Huffington Post, "One quarter of married people are no longer 'in love' with their partner, 15% wish they had married someone else altogether and 3 in 10 have considered ending their marriage or spending time apart." That is a lot of unhappily married folks. But why are individuals so often unsatisfied with their marital partnerships?

Problems in a marriage might stem from dissatisfaction with a spouse or the traditional paradigm of the institution itself. The shiny image of marriage and the promise of love everlasting may have faded. "Marriage is simply nowhere near everything it's been cracked up to be and since we don't need marriage the way we did even 25 years ago, it is in danger of going by the wayside" (Gaduoa, 2017).

I was raised to believe that marriage was not only expected, but necessary. I knew I wanted children, and I never would have considered having kids without a husband to help me raise them. At various times while my children were young, I desperately wanted to leave, but I did not because my belief system demanded that for kids to grow up happy and healthy, they must have a mother and a father who live together. The ominous "broken home" stories I heard throughout my childhood genuinely scared me.

At the time, I believed that if you chose to get married, you were electing to stay that way for the rest of your life. Thankfully, my thinking has evolved over the years, and I no longer entertain such a narrow definition of who should marry, who should raise kids, who should stay married and who should divorce.

Why do we stay in unhappy marriages?

If society no longer shames us into staying married when we are unhappy, why do people still elect to stay in unsatisfying relationships? There are legitimate reasons for staying married, and in this section, we'll touch on some common ones.

Honoring a commitment

Some people just cannot see themselves as divorced individuals. They took a vow and intended to see it through. For these folks, honor holds more value than happiness, and if the marriage is not violent or consistently threatening, its worth might outweigh the potential wreckage that leaving might bring about.

What about the kids?

Despite today's wider acceptance of divorce, some still resist it for the sake of the children. This was certainly true for me. I know current trends advise that divorcing is better for children than watching parents constantly fighting or engaging in other unhealthy relationship behaviors (Neuman, 2014), but for me, the health, well-being, and financial security of my children seemed a monumental obstacle to divorce.

I could not imagine my kids living without their dad in the house. I doubted I could ever make the same amount of money as my husband did. How would I feed and house myself and two growing boys? Once during a particularly difficult time, I called my father for help to leave, knowing that my appeal would likely be rebuffed. As it turned out, I was right. He told me I had made my bed hard and now I had no choice but to lie in it. With no network of support, I did my best to work through the challenges I encountered. However,

27

most of my thinking was stuck in the old paradigm of keeping the marriage together for the kids, no matter what tests or trials life presented.

Once both of my sons were grown, college educated and living on their own, my commitment to sticking with it was no longer about stability for the kids. But I still wanted my marriage to work, so I doggedly kept trying. It was not until I sought outside help for myself that I realized that without change, I would remain in a soul-crushing death spiral. Once I decided to leave, I sought help to get through the logistical details as quickly and painlessly as possible. The equity in the house was separated and I stepped through the rip in my fabric into an unknown world.

As painful as that was, there was one shining light. The wonderful sons that resulted from my marriage explicitly stated that they just wanted me to be happy. If that meant I had to live on my own, they supported my decision. While divorce can be hard on kids, no matter their age, both of my sons have been married themselves and they now understand the challenges of maintaining long-term successful relationships. Nonetheless, "Thank God for my sons," has long been a soothing mantra in my life.

Money and stuff

Some people in unhappy marriages stay because they do not want to give up money or other assets in a divorce settlement (Neuman, 2014). This disincentive to divorce may be stronger for people who have been married a long time than for those who have only been married a few years. Couples who have spent decades together have often built up financial and historical assets and losing money and stuff is often economically and emotionally painful.

Who gets the photographs, the holiday decorations, the memory books? Who wants to give up the lifestyle both parties worked so hard to attain? Who wants to split their monthly income in half, or worse, who wants to lose 50% of their retirement fund? I didn't, but there came a point when losing half of my assets seemed better than losing the rest of my life to what I considered to be an untenable situation.

For homeowners, there is the complication of what happens to the house. Does someone stay, and someone go, or do you sell the house and split the profits? Often, this decision is based on finances more than desire, but the family home is a common reason why people stay married (Neuman, 2014). A house is more than just bricks and mortar – it is the repository for all the memories that were built within those walls.

Leaving our house was certainly an agonizing part of my story. After starting out with precious little and working hard for years to attain a beautiful home, the thought of walking away from the house was devastating. In the end, I decided that the only path available to me was to pick up and move on. Leaving the house and all the friends and neighbors that went with it was one of the toughest decisions of my life. I admit I cried when I left but I know at my core it was the right thing to do.

Who keeps the in-laws?

Another, perhaps surprising, element in the reluctance to leave a marriage is the fear of losing the in-laws (Neuman, 2014). Popular media would have us believe that everyone hates their mother-in-law and that in-laws are a major cause of stress in all marriages; however, for many, this outdated thinking is not true.

It is common to develop loving bonds with members of a spouse's family, and this was undoubtedly true for me. I still love the members of the family into which I married. When I thought about divorcing, the thought of losing contact with them – or worse, having them all mad at me for leaving their brother – was an unappealing prospect. Thankfully, in my case, that did not happen, but for many who face late-in-life divorce, nuclear and extended family ties can be damaged for a time or broken forever.

Dying dreams

When you find yourself in an unhappy union, it is easy to become pessimistic about life in general, and this pessimism is another reason why people stay put (Neuman, 2014). Nursing a negative attitude about life can lead to a breakdown in one's ability to imagine any alternative to the current state of affairs. Even though their dreams may be dying or long dead, some individuals so closely identify as a married person and a family member that they cannot imagine being away from that support system.

For a long time, I stayed married because I worried that I didn't have the logistical skillset or resources to leave and start a life on my own. How does one rent an apartment? How does one file for divorce? Where could I afford to live on my own? Figuring it all out seemed exhausting, so I stayed, knowing I was stuck but lacking the energy or the will to extricate myself.

Clinging to hope

While I went through many moments of unhappiness when I was married, there was another side to the story. There were likewise many wonderful times in my home, which gave me hope that someday things might return to a lighter and better place. The memories of happier moments made me believe that if I had once achieved a level of happiness within the confines of my marriage, I could again. In my heart, though, as I watched what felt to me like a complete breakdown of love and commitment, I knew that improvement was unlikely. I finally had to accept that one person in a partnership cannot make or break a relationship. It truly does take two.

Alone again, unnaturally

At the heart of why I delayed leaving my marriage was my fear of being alone. This sentiment is common among people who have been married a long time. The fear of being alone is born in low self-esteem and a belief that the anticipated state of aloneness will last indefinitely (Neuman, 2014). During my marriage, I had lost objectivity about my self-worth and I had given other people the power to define me. Was I attractive, interesting, funny? I no longer thought so, and I discovered that the inability to find one's own positive attributes leads to feelings of hopelessness and helplessness. I realized I had feared the defining moment of leaving for so long and to such a degree, I no longer felt anything but terror. I was too revolted by my own cowardice to stay, too worried to go.

Over time, my sense of self became deeply damaged, and I knew my own wellbeing was at stake. I suppose as a child I had set in motion the destructive process of subjugating my own needs and opinions to those of other people. If I wasn't a good wife, mother, daughter, sister or coworker, who was I going to be? I had stepped out of my own shoes long ago – so long, in fact, I had forgotten where I had left them. How could I move past this seemingly insurmountable obstacle? I didn't have a ready answer, so I stayed. Evidently, others did too:

> "I knew I needed to leave despite the fact that everything in my background, upbringing, family, and society said 'stay.' I didn't want my children to come from a 'broken' home."
> – Joy Cipoletti (2014)

> "[The] kids were all in college, and I suddenly saw that I was stuck alone with a man who, all those years later, was still wanting me to be someone I wasn't."
> – Barbara Delinsky, *Escape* (2011)

I will give Nora Ephron the last word on why we should remember the raw truths about our relationships. Only fools remember an idyllic past – the rest of us must accept what was real:

> "And then the dreams break into a million tiny pieces. The dream dies. Which leaves you with a choice: you can settle for reality, or you can go off, like a fool, and dream another dream."
> – Nora Ephron, *Heartburn* (1983)

Remembering journaling stem: Examining the rip

Please pause here in your reading to complete the Examining the Rip worksheet at www .reinventioninprogress.com/free-downloads.

Before we can make progress toward a colorful, reinvented future, we must first ground ourselves in honest assessments of our pasts. An accurate and rigorous recording of what happened will allow you to identify what you want to excise from your life as well as the colorful elements you want to infuse into your future.

If you find that you are reluctant to complete a rigorous examination of your past, consider seeking the help of a marriage counselor or therapist. However you choose to examine the rip in your own fabric, honest reflection will help you on your journey. Most of my coaching clients have found that making peace with the honest record of where they have been was a necessary first step in their progression toward reinvention.

TWO
Emotions:
The Blue Thread

If you are like me, remembering brings back lots of smiles and tears. Few marriages are all good or all bad, no matter what gifts or faults each partner brings to the relationship. Most marriages, including mine, are filled with a grab-bag of memories, and those recollections, good and bad, bring up emotions. As we begin to process all the resurrected moments of a relationship past its prime, it's critical that we harness those emotions so they work for us, rather than against any progress we might make.

Getting stuck in any one set of emotions is dangerous when trying to move on from a breakup. Too much sadness can leave us marooned on an island of depression with no lifeboat to assist our return to balance. Too much joy about our newfound freedom can interrupt the natural grief process and lead to a crash of unwelcome and uncomfortable feelings down the road.

How, then, do people properly process emotions after going through a divorce, particularly when the breakup happens later in life? To answer this question for myself, I thought back to other losses I had suffered. How had I coped during those challenging times? I did not want to process my emotions in a stark field of gray, so I returned to my RCAC to find a color that would support me on this part of my journey through the rip in my fabric.

I studied colors and their descriptions, noting my emotional reactions to each. I imagined a thread of each hue loosely encircling me in a safe space. I was seeking a cool color that would allow my grief to surface without swamping me in pain.

For many, blue is the color of depression and sadness, but for me blue is a calming color during stormy times. It is versatile, housing a thousand subtle tones and tints. Blue elicits in me a vision of warm seawater lapping gently against a white sandy beach. When my emotions threaten to overwhelm me, I envision blue to help me reintegrate all the rational and irrational fractals of myself.

When he was about twelve years old, my youngest son made for me a ceramic vase that is still one of my prized possessions. He constructed it using slabs of clay that he formed into an irregular shape made up of both sharp angles and soft curves. It is glazed in translucent Caribbean blue. The base coat is overlayed with whitecap brush strokes and finished with a light sprinkling of small black markings. Unaware of how this talisman would serve me later in life, my son produced a singular piece that perfectly embodied the blue color I needed to conduct a gentle exploration of my breakup emotions.

Surfing

Divorce can be a scary undertaking. Moods can swing in a matter of seconds. Emotional control is difficult to maintain. There are real and imagined losses that can overwhelm the brain's coping mechanisms and engulf common sense. After my divorce, I went through these challenges and their accompanying emotions in waves.

I was, in a word, terrified. I felt like a child again, unable to problem solve and fearful that any decision I might make would move me in the wrong direction. I did not trust myself to make good choices, and every decision I faced brought forth feelings of inadequacy and failure. I was thrust into self-doubt like I had never been before.

Initially, I resisted the need to plunge deep into my emotional well. Although I knew that eventually I would have to explore the depths of my pain, I chose to begin by surfing the waves of my emotions, staying close to the surface as much as I could. However, just like ocean surfers sometimes lose their balance and are swept off their boards by a heaving sea, I often lost my emotional balance and found myself flailing below the surface, unable to take a deep breath or determine which way was up.

I was disoriented as I emerged from these spills looking and feeling like a drowned rat. Although I was initially paralyzed with fear, my dread of floundering eventually outweighed my anxiety about doing something – anything – to disentangle my knot of emotional malaise. I realized that the only way to move forward was to go with the flow, feel everything, and allow the pitching and plunging disequilibrium to swallow me whole. I knew rationally that this head-over-heels feeling would eventually right itself, but not before I fully experienced the instability and vertigo of divorce.

The Six Stages of Grief

In my coaching work over the years, I have listened to hundreds of people describe their feelings of loss and emotional injury. In this work, I often relied upon the easy-to-understand Five Stages of Grief, developed by Elisabeth Kübler-Ross in 1969 and expanded by David

Kessler in 2019 to include a Sixth Stage. As I stepped into my own grief process, I had to remind myself that while the Six Stages of Grief do not present as a linear process, they can be applied to any loss experience in a unique and personal way.

As I traversed the uneven ground of divorce, I experienced denial, anger, bargaining, depression and acceptance, although some people may only go through some of those stages. I knew that Kessler's Sixth Stage – making meaning out of loss – would likely come later for me. I also understood that these stages could recur in any order throughout my grieving process, yet I was still surprised when they did.

The emotions I felt during my ride through the stages hit me with varying degrees of intensity. As I surfed the waters of divorce, my emotions came and went, ebbed and flowed, shoved me down and lifted me up. I did not swim in a straight line through the stages of my own grief.

While living in my utility hotel room, I was clearly in denial. I felt an odd sense of disconnection from the reality of the whole thing. I knew in my head it was happening, but I kept thinking it would end or resolve itself through some miraculous event. I guess I kept hoping against hope that I was just having a bad dream that would fade into hazy memory at a future moment of awakening.

Initially, I believed that my decision to divorce in my sixties must be as rare as a white alligator. I feared I was one of a small number of unlucky or inept people who divorce late in life. However, the sensible side of me, the woman who had been a life coach for three decades, reminded herself that there are few novel experiences in life. If you are going through something that is new for you, chances are someone has already lived it.

I have a strong connection to my spiritual guide and I knew that I would not play *Let's Make a Deal* with my Higher Power. My bargaining-with-God moments were long past me; I had buried them after one too many promises that I would work on improving myself if the powers that be would help me solve the problems I saw in my home. After waiting decades without receiving so much as a whisper of change, I gave up on the notion that the transformation I prayed for might someday come about.

Instead, as I sat in that austere hotel room, contemplating my future life, I raced through my initial denial and jumped quickly into accepting my own need to change. Sometimes, moving forward is the only thing left to do, and over the course of many sleepless nights I realized that I could at least find a different place to live. Feeling somewhat more empowered, I slowly began to look for a home. In those early days, I must have looked at over forty apartments, townhomes and condominiums. After a couple of months, I finally found a place and arranged for a mover to help me get settled.

My days were filled with action, but my emotions swung wildly between acceptance and depression. Each new movement toward freedom brought with it an initial state of euphoria, only to be followed by another dip into the sadness pool. I was not yet able to make meaning out of my divorce or see beyond the immediacy of the pain.

Some people can go through these hardships alone, but I could not. I needed the objectivity of professionals who could help me differentiate the true from the false. I divested myself of the idea that I had all the answers, and I allowed myself to be vulnerable with my professional helpers. I let down my stoic veneer and cried, accepted the depth of my despair, then began to face the bitter truth. With the help of my counselors and support groups, I prepared myself to leave the surface of the pool of sorrow, and with their help, dive deep into the underlying emotions that waited for me below.

Diving deep: Examples of the Six Stages of Grief

The following vignettes illustrate how the Six Stages of Grief might manifest during late-in-life divorces. The stories are fictionalized depictions. They are not representations of my story, nor are they case studies of women I know. Any similarity to anyone living or dead is simply coincidental.

AKIRA'S STORY: DENIAL

When I first left my husband, I was devastated. I was completely gutted that he would be OK with me leaving. I had imagined getting out many times, but now, at fifty-nine, I was shocked that when push came to shove, he was fine with me walking out the door.

I couldn't think of anyone I wanted to confide in about our split, hoping it wouldn't be final. I'd kept the secret of how bad things were from everyone, and if we got back together I didn't want anyone to know that my husband and I were so unhappy. How embarrassing to tell people that for years your marriage has been a lie.

I slept in my car because I didn't have the money for a motel. For the first time in my life, I knew what it must feel like to be homeless. I just drove around, crying and feeling sick. I had a little cash, so I ate fast food and drank a lot of take-out coffee. I kept waiting for my husband to call my cell phone, but he never did.

After a week of living like that, I called a friend who was kind enough to take me in. She, in turn, called several more friends about my situation, and slowly the news of my crumbling home life leaked out. Finally, I broke down and called my brother. He let me stay in his guest room, and my divorce process started from there. I just couldn't believe we were really breaking up. It took a long time for me to accept that I was going to be a divorced person.

JEANIE'S STORY: ANGER

Oh my God, I was so pissed! I spent every waking moment despising my soon-to-be-ex-husband and despising myself for staying so long. Why had I not seen the light years ago and left when I had the chance to start over at a younger age? If I had gone through this at forty instead of sixty, my life could have been so different. I might have found another man to love. I might have gone back to school instead of neglecting my education just to please my husband.

I cry when I get angry, and during those early days I cried all the time. I could not believe I had stayed with a man who told me lies by omission every day for twenty years. I knew he was hiding something. I felt it every time he dodged a question or gave me some half-baked answer when I asked where he had been. Many times, I wondered if there was another woman, but I was shocked when he finally told me he had never honored our monogamous commitment and had been sleeping with several other women for the entire duration of our marriage!

Although I knew in my bones all that time that something was amiss, he never let anyone know who he really was. I felt betrayed, embarrassed and foolish to have placed my faith in such an accomplished liar. I could feel him withdrawing from our marriage for two decades, but I never dreamed that through his silence he was telling such a whopper of a lie. I was furious with myself for suspecting what was happening but failing to be assertive about getting to the bottom of what was going on. What a coward I was!

CHANDANI'S STORY: BARGAINING

I couldn't stand that my husband drank. Despite our religious beliefs about temperance, he drank every day. I guess he was a functional alcoholic because he somehow managed to keep his job as a financial planner. He was the boss, so no one at work ever questioned his behavior or how he looked after a weekend bender.

Only I knew what he was like at home. I'd certainly threatened to leave often enough, but each time I told him I would leave, he laughed at me. He knew I had nowhere to go. Occasionally, after another of my empty threats, he would reduce the amount he drank, but we both knew he could not control it for long. I was hamstrung. After all, the kids were grown and gone, so who was he hurting besides himself? He was not concerned about hurting me, and I realized my feelings had never really counted from the start. I often considered which would be worse – continuing to live with a drunk or being the only divorced woman in my family?

After all my begging and deal-making for him to stop drinking failed, I resorted to prayer. I'm ashamed to admit it, but I asked God to make something happen to his health or his job that would serve as his wake-up call. I prayed that God would give him an ulcer or convince the owner of his company to fire him just to get his attention about his condition, but nothing ever came of my prayer. I promised God that if He would get my husband sober, I would stay with him forever just to hold the family together.

After decades of watching him get worse, I was shocked when one day he announced he was leaving me. I felt guilty about wishing something bad would happen to him, but when he finally left, he said nothing, and I felt nothing but relief.

DANICA'S STORY: DEPRESSION

For a while after my husband asked me to leave, I lived in my sister's basement. I felt like a hollowed-out tree stump. There was nothing left of me but my bark.

I was retired, so I didn't have to get up in the morning – and most mornings, I didn't. In those early days, I slept about sixteen hours a day. I had no energy for anything, and if it hadn't been for my sister forcing me to get up, take a shower and eat, I might have stayed in bed longer than that.

I hated being awake because I cried whenever I thought about him, which was all the time. I guess I'd held in so much during our years together, my tears just leaked out. I was sad that our son didn't call to check on me. I was worried about our daughter because she called too much, always in tears, and always asking me to go home. "Home," I thought. "Where is that for me?"

Sure, we had each played our roles in the disaster I was living, but I thought I had kept up my part of the bargain. I tortured myself by looking back. When had he decided he didn't want me anymore? I wondered how long he had been planning to throw a divorce in my face.

It took me a good three years before I felt anything like normal, and by then I was pushing seventy. I still cannot believe he calmly kicked me to the curb, and I just followed along like a whipped puppy. Every time I looked in the mirror, all I saw was a steaming pile of low self-esteem and regret.

ANITA'S STORY: ACCEPTANCE

Naturally, I suffered when my husband left me for a younger woman. I wondered what I had done wrong. We had been business partners, so I had always contributed financially to our family, but I also did most of the household chores and hauled the kids everywhere they needed to go. I racked my brain, but I couldn't think of anything I had done wrong, except get older.

At first, I foolishly went on a series of radical diets, trying to lose weight and entice him to come home. I exercised like mad, changed my hairstyle and bought new clothes, but rationally I knew these changes were merely cosmetic. There was something wrong with our relationship that ran deeper, but for the life of me I couldn't figure out what it was.

More than once, I drove around at night, trying to spot his car in the parking lots of local hotels or in the driveways of women we knew. On one occasion, I thought I saw him with a woman, only to realize it was someone else when I approached the couple. I honestly don't know what I would have said or done if I had actually ever encountered my husband with someone else. Would I have made a huge scene, thinking that embarrassment might bring him back? I wanted to embarrass him, but I knew that if I did something like that, the only person I would humiliate was me.

A friend insisted I accompany her to a yoga class. At first, I hated it, but I slowly began to recognize I was feeling better. I started meditating and practicing other forms of mindfulness. I began to focus on healing. I got some professional help and did every exercise my therapist suggested. I learned what I could and could not control.

My efforts must have paid off because one day I realized I had not thought about my husband all day. That shocked me. I just didn't care anymore. I was neutral to the whole thing. I knew I would not only survive this experience, but I would learn to thrive on my own. If he wanted someone else, that was his business. I no longer wanted or needed to reengage in a relationship with someone who preferred to be with another.

ELIZABETH'S STORY: MAKING MEANING

When I was sixty-four, my husband and I made a mutual decision to get a divorce. The kids were grown up and we recognized that we no longer had anything in common.

The divorce was painful, like all divorces are, but we both knew we were doing the right thing. We tried to be as fair as we could in separating our assets and debts. Undoubtedly, I was scared. We had been married so long I couldn't imagine life without him. He may have felt the same, but after the divorce was final, we never again spoke about "us."

That was two and a half years ago, and I now feel like all of it makes sense. I had to spend some time away from the man I married so many years ago to see the depth of the rut we were in. Comedians say that tragedy plus time equals comedy, and what a funny pair we had become. We never spent time together because we liked different things. We didn't see eye to eye politically, we didn't like the same people, we didn't enjoy the same activities and even our religious beliefs were now different. In every way, we were not the same people we had been when we got married. It's a wonder we stayed together for as long as we did!

You could say we had grown apart, but all those years ago we had married after a whirlwind romance, so maybe we never really knew each other in the first place. Either way, I now have new friends, a new career and a new man in my life who laughs at what I also think is funny, goes with me to movies and plays we both enjoy and attends political events with me without grumbling about the candidate we're both supporting. What a relief!

Wrestling with angels

Psychotherapist Miriam Greenspan (2003) suggests that:

> "While those who are frightened by the primal energy of dark emotions try to avoid them, becoming more and more cut off from the world at large, those who are willing to wrestle with angels break out of their isolation by dirtying their hands with the emotions that rattle them most."

I was not initially a person who wanted to "wrestle with angels." I wanted to hide in the isolation of my marriage, and I tried to avoid uncomfortable emotions for decades. That's not to say I was never uncomfortable. I certainly was, but during those years I lacked the fortitude to fully engage with the emotional work that needed to be done.

Once I decided to do battle with the divorce angel, my hands got dirty in a hurry. Some days, I felt fine, relieved of the burden of making the decision to leave or stay. I reveled in thoughts about having my own space, deciding how and when to spend my money, and sleeping on the other side of the bed for a change.

Then, without warning, a rogue wave of despair would flood my lifeboat, and I would find myself disoriented in the depths, trying to determine which way was up. Once again, I was lost in a cruel world, feeling just as abandoned as I had felt as a little girl. The Six Stages of Grief were upon me again and the struggle to regain my equilibrium was on.

It was during one of these angelic wrestling matches that I had a revelation. I had been doing everything I could to mitigate my pain. I tried to stay busy and focus on other things. I joined meetups, book clubs and discussion forums. I volunteered. I took classes that I hoped might help me attain new hobbies. I started exercising again, thinking that would help me lose the weight I had gained from months of eating comfort foods.

One day during my workout, I realized I was literally and figuratively running from my life. I was engaging in any activity I could find to distract me from the pain that plagued me. I was desperately seeking a way to circumvent the aching hurt, but nothing was working.

Suddenly, I recalled the words of one of my past mentors. She said many times that the key to going through something difficult is to do just that: Go through. Really feel it. Allow the emotions to wash over you like blue ocean waves. Some of the swells you will encounter will be turbulent and cold, and they may even knock you off your feet; but when they do, get up! Get back on your feet and fight to keep standing. Just go through.

You will never stop the waves of the ocean, but if you are willing to just go through, they will wash you clean and lose their power to undermine your footing. You will get stronger, and the impact of your circumstances will lessen.

Wallowing vs. winning

Divorce can be extremely disorienting, and I felt out of control and powerless. I did not know much about how to survive divorce, but I did know I needed to learn to think more analytically about my situation. How could I overcome the ruin, the utter devastation I felt? How could I restore some measure of control over my life?

I understood that although I was going through a huge upheaval at a decidedly inopportune time, standing still was not an option. The decision to divorce had been made and it was now time to move forward. Staying in the problem would not help – stepping into the solution would.

As both of my counselors advised me, there could be no more running for me. I would have to stand up and go through this experience called divorce. It was suggested that I journal my progress, but I did not want to wallow. I had journaled for years, and when I pulled out some old notebooks and read my entries, I was disgusted with myself. I had repeated the same old story for several decades. That was wallowing, but this time I wanted to win!

I developed my own set of questions that would guide my nightly writing sessions. I wanted to identify my emotions and explore connections between my feelings and the issues I encountered each day. These writing prompts helped me raise my awareness about my progress of "going through" my divorce and they may help you, too. Here is one of my journal entries from early on in my tour through divorce:

SAMPLE JOURNAL ENTRY

Date: August 12, 2019

1. Use three sentences to describe my overall experience today.

    - I slept in, but when I woke up I scrolled through the Internet news.
    - I did my laundry and realized I left my comfy clothes at my old house.
    - I went house-hunting, but still didn't find a place to live.

2. What three emotion words would best describe my overall impressions from today? Use three sentences to describe the triggering event that brought each emotion to the surface.

- Sad:
  - I find news reports depressing, and I feel like I am becoming more and more out of step with the world.
  - I really miss having a place to call home.
  - I saw a couple on the street today, holding hands and chatting comfortably with each other. It made me feel lonely.

- Angry:
  - I'm sitting in this stupid little bedsit while he's living it up in that big house.
  - I am losing so much financially in this deal and I think our mediator is on his side.
  - Knowing how hard this is for me to go through, I don't understand why the kids aren't checking on how I'm doing.

- Fearful:
  - I need to carefully watch my money because this divorce is costing me every dime I have.
  - Each time I look at another apartment that won't work, I wonder if I'll ever find a place to live where I can be safe and comfortable.
  - I'm too old to be starting over at this late stage of life.

3. Stop wallowing and start winning! Given what happened today and the emotions that resulted, how can I change my thoughts or behaviors tomorrow in ways that will lessen the impact of my emotions?

- Set my alarm so I wake up earlier and use the full day to solve today's problems.
- Focus on doing the next right thing.
- Make a list of accomplishments in the evening to remind me of my daily progress.
- Rent a storage unit so I can pick up more of my things.
- Eat three meals over the course of the day and choose more nutritious options.
- Avoid watching or reading the news. I cannot control any of that right now. I will focus only on those things I can control.
- Meditate in the morning and send good thoughts to my children.
- Trust that the kids still love me, but they need time to work through their own feelings as they watch their parents separate.

The point is that divorce is hard, and it is easy to fall into wallowing habits that do not move us forward. To win the wrestling match with the divorce angel, one must fully feel the emotions that the loss caused and allow the "going through" process to unfold.

A final word about "going through"

Divorce is a progression, and we can navigate it in ways that limit our grieving time and help us avoid falling into emotional traps along the way. By naming your feelings, redefining family relationships and adjusting to change, you can eventually find acceptance of your new situation and restore your emotional equilibrium. If you acknowledge divorce as a real bereavement and give yourself permission to feel it as such, you can avoid feeding your resentments, blaming your ex-spouse and acting out your spiteful feelings.

Healing from a divorce takes time and effort, and wallowing will not help you "go through." Feeling the emotions induced by divorce can be uncomfortable and downright agonizing but doing battle with the dark angel of divorce is essential to avoid getting stuck in any one of the Six Stages of Grief.

If you feel like you need professional help or guidance, get it. There are plenty of counselors, support groups and classes designed to help people navigate the logistics and pain of divorce. Take advantage of them. Take whatever steps you need to unload negative emotions and avoid carrying them with you into the fabulous new life you are working to create for yourself. Vow to move through your stages of grief on your own terms and timeline. If you muster the courage to fully immerse yourself in the pool of your emotions, you will emerge a healthier person who is prepared to proceed with the reinvention project that is You.

Emotions journaling stem:
Wallowing vs. winning

Please pause here in your reading to complete the Wallowing vs. Winning journaling stem which can be downloaded for free at www.reinventioninprogress .com/free-downloads. I hope this journaling model helps you stop repeating the same old stories that can bog down writing sessions and keep you stuck in old patterns. You may discover that by actively changing your daily self-talk, you are disentangling yourself from the twists of worn-out emotions while you interlace new ones using threads of a different color.

THREE
Information:
The Red Thread

When I divorced, I had hundreds of jumbled thoughts in my head. Countless memories are made over the course of a long marriage, and although I could remember happy moments, I initially had many more recollections of the bad stuff. Those memories triggered emotions that I had to sort through one by one.

Even though I had known the peace of blue while I explored my feelings, I knew if I stayed in that emotional tumbler I would eventually enter a downward spiral from which I might never recover. It was important for me to remember that emotions do not define who I am, nor are they permanent. Emotions are fickle things that can change with one positive or negative interaction. I did not want the emotions I was feeling – and the distorted thoughts I was having – to become cemented in my brain because I failed to apply reason, logic and information to my feelings.

While emotions can be paralyzing, they can also push us to act when we are otherwise stuck; thus, when I decided to use my feelings to motivate my forward motion, I returned to my RCAC to find the color to represent the stabilizing force of information. Red is associated with anger, and I immediately felt affiliated with it. I saw red every time I thought about all I had lost and why. But red is also the color of excitement, passion, energy and creativity, so I assigned the color red to my search for information.

More importantly than anger, red also represents power and strength. As I began to move out of my emotional state and into one of informed sovereignty, I needed red's vibrancy to step confidently into a future empowered by knowledge. Red inspires a hero's heart, and I would certainly need that as I moved into my next phase of reinvention.

With the power of red in mind, I was struck by a memory of the evening I attended the preschool graduation ceremony of one of my grandsons. I have a photograph of that night, and in it he is giving me the last project he made in preschool: a paper cutout of a superhero whose red shirt reads, "Give Us Hero's Hearts."

That superhero still hangs in my office today. He serves as my red talisman, reminding me to bravely step into new information that has the muscle to transform my emotional self into the empowered heroic woman I want to be. When I see that little superhero, I know that by adding information to the web of my emotions I will embolden my own hero's heart to unpick the tangled knot of confusion that is divorce.

Before the legal aspects of my split were finalized, I embraced the information I attained from lawyers, tax professionals, realtors and bankers. Their expertise was critical in helping me trim away the last tattered shreds of the business end of my married life. However, I needed more information to better understand the connection between my heart and my head. In my thirty-plus years of coaching, I learned how to balance the power of emotion with information, how the brain functions under stress, and how change impacts thinking. Perhaps I could use some of that information now to mitigate my own emotional journey.

Change, transition and stress

It is well documented that change, even good and expected change, causes stress in our brains – and consequently in our bodies (Kaufer and Kirby, as cited by Sanders, 2013). Our ability as human beings to effectively handle the stress that change produces affects every aspect of our lives; therefore, it is helpful to monitor our stress levels, particularly when we are facing a major life change like divorce.

Good stress, otherwise known as *eustress* (Selye, 1983), is brought on by small, manageable changes that a person sees as a stretch of their current competencies, yet achievable. Eustress is good for people. It motivates us to learn, evolve, achieve, invent, inquire and engage with daily challenges.

Eustress allows teachers to create lessons that motivate students to move from one level of performance to the next. In ideal situations, each challenge induces a manageable level of stress for students, but not so much stress that learners feel out of their depth. A level of stress that is too high creates *distress* (Selye, 1983), which shuts down a learner's ability to accept new challenges and move forward.

The notion of eustress is fundamental to our understanding of how we humans navigate paths of physical or emotional transition from one condition to another. We have already examined the Six Stages of Grief (Kübler-Ross, 1969; Kessler, 2019), which is a change model focused on loss. The Six Stages model posits that we encounter a newly induced state of intense grief (high stress) and move through a series of stages (denial, anger, bargaining, depression, acceptance and making meaning) to achieve a reduced or moderated state of grief (reduced stress).

In 1991, William Bridges created a transition model for managing change. Bridges' work is widely applicable and shows that change alone does not trip us up – it is the *transition process* the change triggers that produces stress.

Change is an *external and situational* event that happens to an organization or individual. Divorce, whether you initiated it or not, is a perfect example of an external change, while transition, the process of "going through," is internal. Change happens *to* us, but transition is an *inside job*: our own reinvention process represents the internal transition that results as we actively engage with the change of divorce.

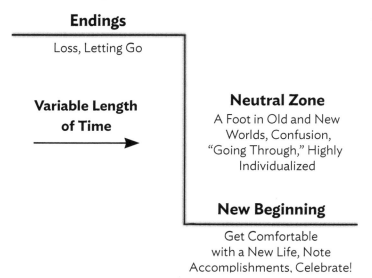

Endings, The Neutral Zone, and New Beginnings
(The Bridges Transition Model, 1991)

Endings

Endings can be painful (Bridges, 1991). So painful, in fact, we often delay them until long after a natural culmination should have taken place. The end connotes suffering, shock, and a feeling of incongruity between the known and the unknown. Life-altering endings such as a job loss, death of a loved one, or divorce may produce unintended consequences for our brains and bodies that can ripple for weeks, months or years.

The impact of an ending often hinges on how much an individual is involved in determining that a change is necessary. Our responses to endings likewise depend on how invested we are in the way things used to be; thus, transitioning through change is easier for some people than others.

Some folks seem to sail through big life changes. These are the people who throw divorce parties and glide through the transition of losing a spouse with ease. These individuals are referred to as "early adopters" by Everett Rogers in his 2003 book, *Diffusion of Innovations*. When an early adopter faces a personal or professional change, they meet it with open arms and attitudes. Early adopters are not afraid of transition or change because they believe – either innately or based on past experience – that they have the capacity to meet any challenge and successfully navigate uncharted waters.

Early adopters also do not perceive change as negative. They recognize that positive outcomes can come from changing themselves and their circumstances. Thus, they approach the ending of how things used to be with a can-do attitude. Early adopters do not prolong finales – they cut the cord and make a conscious decision to jump straight into the future.

People all over the world often formally mark endings with an event or a set of actions: We have a closing ceremony for the Olympics. We hold funerals to celebrate the lives of people who have died. We have graduation ceremonies for students leaving school and retirement parties for workers winding up their careers. These are all acknowledgments that an ending has taken place and closed a chapter in someone's life.

My acceptance of the end of my marriage came on the day I went through a box full of old birthday and anniversary cards, notes, emails and valentines. I tore through these expressions of a worn-out love and cast them into the trash as I said goodbye to the date and year written on each one. The scraps of paper were nothing in and of themselves, but they were symbols of the care and devotion I once believed in. I cried over each item in that box and finally acknowledged the ending. After that, I knew I could never go back to my old home, and I entered the Neutral Zone of my divorce.

The Neutral Zone

All change processes require you to spend some time in the Neutral Zone (Bridges, 1991) between what used to be and what you want in the future. During this time, it is normal to feel like you're living in freefall, but the Neutral Zone also provides an opportunity for you to take a cold hard look at your previous circumstances and at the emotions you felt at the end. The Neutral Zone offers an opening to cut lines of communication with your past and create new ties to your future.

When you are in the Neutral Zone, you are in the middle, and the instability of the transition can be overwhelming. At this stage, it is important to resolve that the ending is permanent and going back is not an option. The middle is often uncomfortable, and the temptation to try to climb back up to where you were can be strong. But hold firm. It may feel like you are plummeting into the pit of the unknown, but now is the time to step out in faith. You are taking solid action to create and solidify a vision of the new reality you want for yourself.

Again, early adopters (Rogers, 2003) have an advantage in the Neutral Zone. They don't like being stuck in the middle. In fact, they do not like being stuck anywhere, so they force themselves to progress through the Neutral Zone, exploring their options and moving quickly through their own transitions.

The Neutral Zone in the Bridges model shown earlier in this chapter is represented by a vertical line that drops from the Ending line to the line of New Beginning. For early adopters, this vertical line can be drastically shortened because people who deal with transition well move through the change process at a faster rate. Conversely, when people get trapped in the Neutral Zone, they unconsciously delay the internal work they need to do by focusing on a host of outside fixes that will not repair the damage that has been done. They want to restore the old way, rather than working to acknowledge a new reality. Inevitably, even people who get stuck in the Neutral Zone eventually must accept that their only way out is "going through." They will ultimately come to a New Beginning, but they may be dragged there by life, kicking and screaming.

As I was moving through my divorce, I often struggled with seeing my own progress through the Neutral Zone. I felt like I was on a treadmill endlessly walking but getting nowhere. I was besieged by depression and, even though I had good days and bad days, I struggled to keep track of all that was happening. I was grieving the outside change that had happened to me, but I was determined to do the inside work of transition. I realized I needed a tool to help me stay in the solution and monitor my headway.

I decided to periodically take stock of where I had been, what I had accomplished and where I was going. The following excerpt from my journal lists the accomplishments I made over the first six months of my divorce process.

MY SIX-MONTH LIST OF ACCOMPLISHMENTS

- Met with a mediator
- Prepared divorce documents
- Endured living in utility hotel for three months
- Bought a house
- Hired movers
- Supervised my move
- Packed my things
- Shopped for and replaced things left behind
- Unpacked everything and set up a new house
- Added landscaping to my back yard
- Met new neighbors and started new friendships
- Adopted a dog
- Changed my hairstyle
- Installed my alarm system
- Worked through getting new health insurance
- Updated my retirement plan
- Updated my will
- Hosted two sets of house guests
- Installed a doorbell camera
- Ordered window coverings
- Put up Christmas decorations
- Visited my son for three weeks
- Added air to my car tires

- Hired a company for snow removal
- Had the oil changed in my car
- Joined a support group for writers
- Installed "smart" lights
- Took my dog to training classes

Your list will undoubtedly differ from mine. My list may not seem long to you, but to me it demonstrated survival and progress. I realized I was indeed "going through." While none of the items on my list indicated that I had fully arrived at my New Beginning, they were reminders that I was "going through" the Neutral Zone and creating distance between me and the Ending.

The New Beginning

The New Beginning (Bridges, 1991) is the desired destination for reinventors, yet it is not where the work of your progress ends. It is the point at which you can begin to realize your reinvented purpose, your vision, your plan. Having completed your journey through the Neutral Zone, you can start afresh.

At your point of New Beginning, you are free to nurture yourself in new and unexplored ways. You will redefine the core values that will guide the choices you make. You will envision the life you want for yourself and you will decide who you want to include in your network of supportive people. You will engage with time in new ways, and you will dedicate the time you have to actualize each color of the new life fabric you have designed for yourself.

Once you have arrived at a New Beginning, you will be able to tell yourself and others your truth. While developing your plan is solitary work, now is the time to let others begin to see the reinvented you.

As I added my red threads to the new fabric of my life, it felt risky to reveal the reinvented Me; however, showing my initial changes to the world allowed me to begin to express the person I wanted to be. I stepped into my New Beginning and gifted myself a moment to admire the garment I was intertwining with the fresh colors of my reinvention. I began to distance myself from the rip in my old fabric, and I knew deep inside that I would be alright. I could accept my new pattern with grace, knowing that it would be led by providence and by plan.

The stressed-out brain

The medical community has learned much over the past forty years about how the brain and body work together to respond to stress. In an attempt to help us better understand how brain and body chemistry react to stressors, Harvard Medical School published an article titled "Understanding the Stress Response: Chronic Activation of this Survival Mechanism Impairs Health" (2020). When we experience stress, the amygdala, the segment of the brain responsible for emotional response, partners with the hypothalamus to send out chemical signals to the body to respond to stressful situations. These distress signals stimulate psychological and physiological responses that propel us to stand our ground or run.

Most of us know of the "fight, flight or freeze" responses, but many of us are less familiar with the amygdala's ability to hijack the brain's normal processing function. When the brain perceives a threat, the amygdala acts as the gatekeeper for the brain. Hormones are released that warn the parts of the brain designed to respond to danger, and, from there, they take control of the body's chemistry and actions.

The amygdala is our friend when we are about to be hit by a car or being chased by a tiger, but there is a downside to this rapid response system. While this urgent hormonal communication is going on in the amygdala, hypothalamus and adrenal systems, the parts of the brain that provide executive functions like problem solving, creativity and a sense of control are blocked from being fully engaged. The amygdala shuts the gate on those functions because it perceives that the body is in imminent danger and nothing else matters at that moment (Harvard Medical School, 2020).

As emotions rise and fall over the months or years required to successfully navigate a divorce, we can find ourselves in a constant state of fight, flight or freeze, meaning that the brain's – and subsequently the body's – response to stress is always being triggered by a cascading release of hormones. This process, when experienced over an extended period, can lead to chronic stress (Harvard Medical School, 2020).

From my work with children who have emotional disorders as well as with stressed-out adults, I have witnessed the amygdala hijack in action many times. However, my recent experience with divorce was now forcing me to consider the adverse long-term effects of chronic stress on my own body and brain. I realized that information – the red thread – could help me lessen the impact of my emotions and the potential damage of chronic stress resulting from my own amygdala hijack.

Complex post-traumatic stress disorder

What happens when abuse or neglect are part of the present or past experiences of someone going through a divorce? In his 2014 book titled *Complex PTSD: From Surviving to Thriving*, Pete Walker describes complex post-traumatic stress disorder (CPTSD) as a condition that commonly results from repeated childhood experiences of physical abuse or neglect. Children whose families are unable or unwilling to meet their needs can experience overwhelming feelings of unworthiness due to verbal, emotional, spiritual, sexual, and/or physical abuse or abandonment. These kids are at increased risk of developing CPTSD.

Although I was physically punished as a child, I do not remember experiencing extreme physical or emotional abuse. However, I have certainly imported into my adult life the effects of the emotional abandonment I did go through. The physical and emotional needs of the other members of my family of origin were so high, many of my childhood needs were sublimated or ignored.

I don't blame anyone for this; but it did happen, and it drove home for me the notion that my emotional needs were insignificant and unimportant compared to others'. The results of my unmet childhood needs were an inability to trust other people, an overwhelming need to keep the lid on stressful situations and an intense fear of being abandoned. These notions have impacted every relationship in my life. In many ways, they created an easily triggered monster who does not have relationships at all, but instead takes hostages.

Trauma and shame

Physical or emotional abandonment experienced in childhood often burdens victims with what John Bradshaw (1988) described as "toxic shame." While healthy shame allows us to make mistakes and gives us "permission to be human" (p. 24), unhealthy or "toxic shame" makes one "believe that *[their] whole self is fundamentally flawed,* and defective" (emphasis in original, p. 37).

Shame prevents us from developing a strong sense of self-esteem. It can also produce anxiety and depression while constraining our ability to connect with others in healthy relationships. Unlike feeling guilty about *doing* something wrong, shame is experienced as *being* something wrong (Bradshaw, 1988, p. 38).

It took years of self-examination and recovery work for me to recognize my own CPTSD and toxic shame as two of my internalized motivators for staying in my marriage as long as I did. I lacked a strong sense of self when I got married, so when the going inevitably got tough, I was frequently triggered by old emotional injuries and shamed by my perceived inability to fix disagreements. I continually blamed myself for problems that arose in my home, and, over time, I became less of my authentic self.

In addition, I developed a textbook case of codependency as described by Robin Norwood in her 1985 book *Women Who Love Too Much: When you keep wishing & hoping he'll change.* Like the women Norwood's book describes, I had a "fragile self-image" (p. 10) and I became "more and more dependent on [my husband] and [our] relationship in order to feel good" (p. 14–15).

I was addicted to my partner and the thought of losing him triggered my emotional insecurity in every way imaginable. As my parents experienced a generation before, I saw that my life was vulnerable to the negative impact of some innocuous event that would suddenly trigger long periods of silence or verbal discord. When these events arose, I found myself reduced to reliving the shame and powerlessness of my childhood. Those old feelings of inadequacy would return, and I would retreat into my hole of isolation and despair.

When I discovered that I was a raging co-dependent and filled with toxic shame, I was abashed. I felt overwhelmed and deficient, yet there was some relief in knowing that I could heal if I could complete an honest remembrance of my childhood and apply new information about CPTSD, toxic shame and codependency. If I could understand these terms and accept how they applied to my life, I had a chance to recover and reinvent myself.

As I continued to work through the memories and emotions of my marriage and divorce, I made a conscious choice to take action. I needed to reduce my stress while going through the sensitive work of remembering and processing the emotions of my divorce. To accomplish a reduction in stress I needed to apply all I had learned about CPTSD, toxic shame and codependency. Some of the strategies I tried were more successful than others, but if you are struggling with this critical work I suggest the following:

1. **Seek help from a pro.** Professional counselors and therapists are knowledgeable about the ins and outs of divorce and the churning emotions it produces. They can help you look honestly at your past, survive the present and develop a set of goals for the future.

2. **Lean on your support network.** Our friends and family are often our best defense against sinking into panic, despondency or depression. If you are not close with any family members or friends, join a support group or take a class on divorce recovery. Sharing your burden with others is a great way to lessen its weight.

3. Learn and regularly practice **methods of mindfulness.** These meditative activities, which might include meditation, yoga, tai chi, prayer, visualization and controlled breathing, help slow racing thoughts and create inner peace.

4. Engage in **physical activity** to the point where you break a sweat. Getting physical helps you release negative emotions like toxic shame, anger and fear. Physical movement likewise facilitates freedom from the law of inertia as it applies to the body and the mind.

5. **Journal.** By using the Wallowing vs. Winning journaling stem from Chapter 2, you can enhance your sense of control and regain power over your thoughts, words and actions. However, whether this form of journaling works for you

or not, journal anyway. By putting pen to paper, you will clarify your thoughts, process feelings, dream bigger dreams, and create plans for making those dreams come true.

6. **Avoid isolation**. Even if you don't feel like it, force yourself to plan social contact with friends and acquaintances. Consider stepping out of your comfort zone to do something new or resume an activity you haven't done in years. Taking low-stakes risks in the social domain can help you regain your confidence and acquire new interests.

Learned helplessness

Relationships in which one or both partners carry CPTSD, shame or codependence, can lead to the development of "learned helplessness," a term coined by Seligman and Maier in 1967. Learned helplessness is the prison of the mind. It induces vulnerable individuals to stay in a cage built by another, even after the door has swung wide open. Learned helplessness emerges when an individual continues to live in an unhealthy or uncontrollable situation, giving up on the notion that change is possible, even when faced with evidence to the contrary.

When I was married, I was assuredly locked up in a prison cell of my own making. I tried to get up the courage to leave on multiple occasions, but I always returned thinking somehow this time might be different. I was stuck, and I was baffled. For reasons I could not see, I was able to perform competently – even powerfully – at work but was unable to comport myself as that same person at home. My outside image was strong, but my inside confidence was weak, and the longer I stayed, waiting for things to change, the harder it was to walk away.

However, there is hope. It is by remembering the truth, understanding one's emotions and gaining awareness through information that reinventing women can regain their connection to their heroic hearts and acquire the strength to rebuild a life and reinvent their future.

Information journaling stems

Stem 1: The Neutral Zone

Making it through the Neutral Zone is challenging, and it is often difficult to track the steps you've taken that prove that you are indeed making progress. I invite you to fill out the Neutral Zone List of Accomplishments which can be downloaded for free at www.reinventioninprogress.com/free-downloads.

Stem 2: CPTSD, codependency
and learned helplessness

You can find references regarding CPTSD, codependency and learned helplessness, as well as information about how to find help at https://www.reinventioninprogress .com/free-downloads.

FOUR
Nurturing:
The Green Thread

To nurture is to feed, to teach, or to develop someone or something with tenderness and love. All human beings are born with a need to be nurtured. Babies must be fed and kept clean and warm. They must know the comfort of human touch and hear the voice of a loving caretaker. They must be taught how to walk and talk, how to love and be loved, how to play and have fun, how to read, and how to master self-care skills so they are prepared to move through childhood and into a healthy adolescence and adulthood. Being nurtured early in life lays the foundation for developing physical strength, mental toughness and spiritual inspiration. Nurturing leads to resilience.

Resilience is the ability to bounce back after going through a traumatic situation. It comes from an inner strength, a resolve to remain undeterred, even when life hands us a misfortune or disaster. Applying the terms of the Bridges model (1991), resilience is the ability to confront an Ending, to fight through the Neutral Zone and arrive at a New Beginning ready to do the ongoing work of reinvention. Learning to nurture resilience is central to the healing process necessary for all human beings when we suffer a loss like divorce.

Resilience gained from self-nurturing provides the freedom to be one's authentic self. It offers a set of goals and behaviors that prepare us to roll with the punches, recover our footing, and push through to the other side of pain. It is the mental, physical and spiritual work that gives us the inner resources to deal with the hardships of life.

I must admit that I have not always been good at nurturing myself or willing to accept nurturing from others. As a child, I was taught that if you want something done, you should do it yourself. Right or wrong, I did not learn about teamwork in my family of origin; in that environment, the need for assistance signaled weakness. There have been many times over the course of my life when I would have rather died than ask someone for help. I do not say this proudly – my radical self-reliance has taken me to some dark mental and emotional places.

However, when I divorced I was occasionally forced to rely on others for help. I could not lift all the boxes I packed, move the furniture I took or deal with my own emotional turmoil by myself. When I finished moving, I met up with a friend who had been keeping my dogs for me during the process. After we got the pups settled in my SUV, she reached back into her car and handed me a lovely copper pot that contained an arrangement of succulents. My eyes filled with tears and she gave me a hug. She reminded me that I was like a succulent: a resilient person who could withstand anything. I realized at that moment that my new plant would serve as my talisman for resilience, and I would add a green thread to the tapestry of my reinvention.

Succulents are one of nature's most extreme examples of resilience. They live in harsh, dry conditions, but they can store enough water to survive long periods of drought. They have thick skin and thorns to ward off the heat of the desert and the assaults of predators, as well as water-storing roots to help them survive flash floods. But succulents do not just survive. Many varieties produce flowers even under severe conditions, proving that true strength and beauty come from inside and are not solely dependent on external conditions.

The succulent collection my friend gave me that day is still the only house plant I have. It has thrived and holds a prominent place in my kitchen. I see those engorged green tendrils of aloe vera every morning as I'm pouring my first cup of coffee, and, as time has passed, my succulents have become my daily reminder that the choice to thrive must be regularly reinforced. They have served as verdant threads for my new fabric, green tendrils of life that inspire my ongoing work to nurture my own resilience.

Laying my foundation for resilience

During the time leading up to my divorce, and going through the process itself, I sometimes felt resentful that I had spent so much of my life – nearly my entire life – taking care of other people.

When I was growing up, my mother had muscular sclerosis, which was difficult to diagnose and more difficult to treat. She had intermittent symptoms typical of the disease. She struggled with balance, generalized muscle deconditioning and emotional control. My father was impatient with her illness and demanded that she not embarrass him by dragging a leg or falling. Once when she was driving, she was pulled over by a police officer and given a roadside sobriety test. As you might expect, she nearly failed the assessment because of her unsteady gait and inability to stand on one foot. When Dad found out about that, he was enraged.

In addition, my older sister was born with a birth defect that required lots of painful therapy and several difficult surgeries. Of course, my parents did everything they could to help her recover from those procedures both physically and emotionally. In addition, they directly and indirectly made me a part of her treatment plan.

My first job at the age of seven was to wait alone for hours in hospital lobbies while my mother sat with my sister upstairs. Although I dreaded those long stretches of time alone, I was allowed to bring a tall stack of books to keep me company. It was during those slow days that I developed a love of reading. While waiting for my mother to return, I could travel to different worlds, imagine myself as Florence Nightingale, or immerse myself in the trials and tribulations of *The Hundred and One Dalmatians*.

At that time, children were not allowed to visit their siblings in hospitals because it was feared that they would carry into a sterile environment the germs that caused childhood illnesses like measles, chicken pox and mumps. Back in the dark ages of the 1960s, this was a real possibility, and otherwise healthy kids were the natural enemies of sick children. Today, thanks to vaccines, kids are no longer perceived to be so threatening.

Even without factoring in my mom's and my sister's conditions, my father's chronic depression always needed care. My second job was to cheer him up, and I literally tap-danced for him on occasion. I became the merry prankster in the house. For some reason, I could approach Dad, even when no one else could. I loved to sneak up on him as he fixed things at his work bench, just to see if I could startle him or get a reaction. If I could get Dad to laugh, even once, the ice around his heart would begin to melt and he would initiate his slow assent back to the world of the living.

Understandably, these physical and mental challenges created tremendous stress in our house. No one was to blame, but my mother and father never learned from their families of origin how to nurture themselves. They knew how to "white knuckle" life, and their ability to endure hardship was obvious, but they did not practice good habits of self-care, self-compassion or creative problem solving. They did the best they could with the skills they had, but unfortunately my parents were excellent role models for CPTSD and codependency. By the time I met and married my spouse, I was already living a dysfunctional lifestyle built on unreasonable expectations, blame, isolation and toxic shame. I had no idea how to nurture myself.

The good news was that by the time I divorced, I had enough life experience to know that bouncing back from trauma and shame was possible. I got to know other people who were nurturing to others and to themselves. Many of my friends and colleagues demonstrated inner strength, open-minded attitudes and self-love, and I wanted that for myself as well. I watched how people who held firmly to their personal power nurtured themselves and I simply copied what they were doing.

Several of my assistants swore by massage therapy as a way to release tension and gain inner peace. One year for my birthday, they bought me a gift certificate for an hour-long massage at a swanky spa. By the end of that hour, I was a convert. I could not believe how good I felt – and, naturally, I wanted more of that feeling.

At the same time, the woman who cleaned my house also taught yoga. She had been telling me about the benefits of yoga and meditation for years, so I decided to try it. Again, I was stunned by the results. I felt stronger emotionally and physically, and I began to feel more in control of my reactions to the chaos in my life.

On the advice of a friend, I took a course that taught meditation as a form of spiritual connection to myself, my Higher Power and the universe. Using this meditation method as a doorway, I began to work holistically on my beliefs about myself, my family, my friends and the world at large. After practicing meditation and prayer for several years, I was ready for my next step.

I reached a point where I was able to fully embrace remembering what happened in my past and feeling my true emotions about my childhood and my marriage. Although I had studied the attributes of resilience years earlier, it was not until I faced the truth about my own past and present that I was ready to move on toward my own bouncing back. I was beginning to recognize that, throughout my past difficulties, I had repeatedly demonstrated that – by accident or intention – I had become a resilient person.

Who is steering my ship?

Early in my education career, I started an alternative high school for kids with special emotional and behavioral needs. Many of my students had track records of school failure. Through episodes of substance abuse, destructive behavior and self-harm, they screamed to the world that they did not like who they were. I began to research ways to help my students cultivate greater stress tolerance and rebound strength. I discovered the concept of resilience as I was trying to understand the connection between learned helplessness and poor performance in school.

The kids in my school often blamed their parents, friends, or teachers for their poor performance and past failures. Many of my students – and, interestingly, some of their parents – perceived schools as hostile places. Over years, and sometimes generations, of failure with school systems, they formed beliefs that they had little or no control over their interactions with institutions or other people. Individuals who hold these beliefs about themselves and the world exercise an external locus of control (Cherry, 2019).

When operating with an external locus of control, people often place responsibility for their successes or failures on reasons outside of themselves such as luck or the good or bad will of others. My students pointed fingers at a lot of people, and helping them to own their own behaviors and outcomes became paramount in our work together. Resilience training became the order of the day. If self-nurturing leads to greater resilience, how does one go about learning those skills?

Learning to be resilient

Learning to be resilient may be the greatest gift we can give ourselves. To become resilient, we must invest time in learning a set of behaviors and thought patterns that foster bounce-back abilities in the mind, body and spirit. We must learn to love ourselves, warts and all – at the very least, to the level at which we love other people.

Building resilience means we learn ways to be kind to ourselves. We commit to becoming the champions of our own plans and efforts. We are required to examine the content of our self-talk and stop sending ourselves negative messaging long after the people who taught us to talk that way are gone. We must live with a spirit of open-mindedness and be willing to see a broader context for living. Perhaps most importantly, to develop resilience we must nurture deep gratitude that focuses our thoughts on all that we have, rather than that which we currently lack.

The resilient mind

Mental resilience results when an individual faces a challenge great enough to capture the mind's full attention. Fear of failure, a significant loss or a stunning defeat are sufficiently shocking to inspire humans to transcend our past beliefs and discover our true reasons for living. The brain sometimes requires a jolt to move from a passive state into an active state in which a new calling can be uncovered. Calamity can serve as our wake-up call to show us that hardship can release hidden genius (Steinberg, 2015).

If we accept this idea of resilience building, misfortunes like divorce are the mettle-testing heat we must survive to cement our belief that a problem exists, and that we are the ones to fix it. Through this process, we forge a new course of action which is aligned with our desire to improve an untenable situation. Once we are convinced that we alone hold the solution to a seemingly unsolvable problem, we have established a foothold on mental resilience (Steinberg, 2015).

We can also foster the ability to bounce back by serving others. When we extend a hand of service to our community, we offer hope and help to someone who is worse off than we are. By giving of our time and talents to others, we nurture our own feelings of empowerment and develop heightened gratitude for our blessings (Scott, 2020).

Individuals who are mentally tough take a long-range approach to life. Like the "early adopters" described by Rogers (2003), mentally resilient people do not believe that their current problems or state will last forever. They remember that change is guaranteed in life and that uncomfortable circumstances will eventually end.

They likewise passionately believe they possess the power and skill to affect positive change and that they can spread their optimistic thinking to others. The mentally resilient among us focus on shifting their self-talk to an affirmative tone, and, by doing so, they remind the rest of us that hardships are merely temporary inconveniences.

Mental resilience requires us to accept problems with grace. The mind of a resilient person acknowledges that their life story, up to this point, is in the books. It cannot be changed, but resilient thinkers focus on lessons learned and insist that future action can be different. They have hope that positive change is waiting just around the corner, and they believe they have at least a modicum of control over transforming a troublesome present into a constructive future (Scott, 2020).

People who successfully overcome challenges often look for ways to extract meaning from difficult situations (Frankl, 1962). Although Viktor Frankl spent three years in Nazi concentration camps during World War II, he noted in his book, *Man's Search for Meaning: An Introduction to Logotherapy*, that individuals who find value in their life events, even when those events cause tremendous suffering, can transcend tragic circumstances and overcome obstacles: "In some way, suffering ceases to be suffering at the moment it finds a meaning..." (p. 135). No matter what difficulty we are enduring, if we can attach meaning to the experience, we can truly "go through" it with grace.

When we become resilient people, we become values driven, and the capriciousness of life does not easily derail us. We must learn to depersonalize our experiences. We cannot take every change in life as a personal affront; we must roll with the punches, understand the situation is temporary and humbly believe that we can overcome whatever comes our way. For the mentally resilient person, life is an ever-changing carnival ride where nothing should be taken too seriously (Scott, 2020).

The resilient body

When my grandmother was my age, she was considered elderly. I suppose during my youthful years I thought of anyone over thirty as old, but my grandmother was already declining into inactivity in her sixties. She did not take walks. She certainly did not run or ride a bike. The heaviest weight she lifted was her cast-iron skillet. She did some light housework, but she avoided the heavy lifting by inviting her host of grandchildren to stay at her house. She loved spending time with us, but part of the deal was that we youngsters would complete the more demanding chores in her home before anything fun started. I loved my grandmother dearly, but I never thought of her as a physical dynamo. She played a mean game of pinochle, but I could never have imagined her running a 5k, doing yoga or practicing relaxation strategies.

In her defense, attitudes about aging were different in Grandma's day. She never expected to stay active well into her seventies, eighties and nineties. But today, technology and research have helped us form new attitudes about nutrition, movement, exercise and cardiovascular health. As human life expectancy has increased in the West, older people have changed their outlook on maintaining a high-quality life well past the point when Grandma had settled into her rocking chair.

With every advancement in health and wellbeing, we learn more about the strong relationship between the mind and the body; thus, as we look at improving the resilience of the mind, we must also exercise our physical muscle of resilience. Spirituality and health journalist Kalia Kelmenson (2020) agrees that human beings need to give proper credit to the work our bodies do for us every day. She explains that "Creating resilience in our body allows us to recover faster from any setbacks we have."

To be physically resilient, we must develop habits that exercise the muscles, bones and soft tissues that allow us to bounce back from stress, injury or illness. We nurture our bodies and improve our resilience when we embrace weight-bearing activities that involve movement and balance. And just as our minds need love, attention and intellectual stimulation, our bodies need proper nutrition to function at top capacity. As we age, our bodies require more activity and less calorie-dense foods. A healthy diet not only affects how we feel physically but also how we function mentally – it is just as important as a healthy and balanced physical exercise routine.

We all want to feel good for as long as we can, but how can we best preserve our fluidity of movement and physical resilience as we strive to live life to the fullest over the next ten, twenty, thirty or forty years? By examining how we sit, stand, lift and walk, and by listening to our bodies' reactions as manifested by discomfort, energy levels, pain and appearance, we can determine when we need to improve the ways in which we physically move through the world. To make this assessment, we must first address the structural integrity of our own bodies.

Maintaining structural integrity involves holding the body in the correct posture and using proper body mechanics for everyday functional tasks. Our posture is a direct expression of the messages the mind and body are sending back and forth. When our energy is low or we feel unsafe, our bodies seek a protective stance. In this state, the body may tend to slouch with the head bowed and the shoulders pulled forward. The body naturally isolates and insulates itself against perceived threat or assault (Kelmenson, 2020).

When we notice we are taking on a slouching posture, we can exercise our resilience muscles by standing up straighter, opening the chest and stacking the joints in proper alignment (Kelmenson, 2020). Correct stacking is a concept in yoga and other physical practices that honor the mind-body connection. It begins with a firm foot plant, usually by imagining the foot as a four-point platform. The ball of the foot provides two points, and the heel provides two additional points. Next, by placing our feet shoulder width apart, we provide a balanced foundation allowing the body to align in a stacked position.

The aim of stacking is to balance the weight of the body evenly. The feet should be aligned under the ankles, the ankles planted firmly under the knees and the knees aligned under the hips. The back, shoulders, neck and head should be stacked over the hips in an erect and aligned position. By focusing on how we stand and complete functional everyday tasks, we can avoid injury and create greater inner space for our movement, bodily processes and thinking capacity. Good body alignment gives us the strength to better oxygenate our cells, digest our food, and stimulate healthy blood and lymphatic flow.

The resilient spirit

Our minds and bodies are storehouses for stress. When we live with chronic stress from life experiences such as trauma, unhealthy relationships, loss and divorce, we hold the stress these events produce throughout our bodies. These pockets of old stress may not reveal themselves for years, and we often don't realize that they are causing us pain. They become encased in layers of scar tissue as the body and mind attempt to move on or refuse to face the horrors of the past. Old stress may manifest as physical or mental illness, pain, fatigue and/or a generalized malaise. The list of negative outcomes from unresolved stress is endless.

Although chronic stress creates havoc in the mind and the body, perhaps most importantly, chronic stress is also soul-crushing. Therefore, I believe it is important to reduce stress by strengthening our spiritual connectedness to powers that exist on nonlinear and invisible planes.

Spirituality means different things to different people. Although some rely on a religious practice for their spiritual nutrition, the investment in spirituality is often separate from religious rituals. Many atheists recognize that they are not the center of the universe and, like their religious or agnostic fellows, seek to better understand how they fit in the grand scheme of things (Atwood, 2012). To achieve spiritual resilience, most of us need to believe in something bigger than ourselves to become fully self-actualized, but this does not require belief in a traditional God or supreme being.

We can reach greater heights in our individual spirituality by honoring our own worthiness and accepting that we are more than accidents of the cosmos or flukes of nature. We may each be but a tiny particle of dust on the Earth, which is in turn a tiny speck in our galaxy, which is but a fleck in the universe, but that does not mean we are too small to sense our complex interconnectedness with each other. We all share an existential human bond that is greater than each of us individually. To embrace our spiritual resilience, we must accept that we each hold an important place in the great network of life on this planet.

In my late twenties, I was re-entering the workforce after having my second child, and I decided to take a class for women in my position to spruce up my resume and gain insight about my interests and talents. One of our assignments was to make a list of the top thirty priorities in our lives. Unsurprisingly, my list included my children, marriage, family, health, financial wellbeing and home. It took me about five minutes to list thirty items that were priorities in my life.

After we made our lists, the instructor asked us to raise our hand if we had placed ourselves and our spirituality in the top ten items on our list, and suddenly, I had a sinking feeling. I could not raise my hand for the first ten items, nor for the second or the third. I did not appear on my own list at all, nor did my spiritual life. I was not #1. I was not even #30.

It shocked me that while making my list, it never occurred to me that I should be on it, nor that my spiritual connectedness was essential to my own well-being. At that point in my life, I did not even know how to spell "self-care" and I certainly was not spiritually grounded.

Even though at that time I was a practicing Catholic, my spiritual resilience was weak. I believed that my sons were children of God and that my husband was a sanctified being, but the list I made that day was clear evidence that I did not believe that I too, was God's child, and I recognized that I had some spiritual work to do.

Spiritual resilience only requires that we accept our own humanity, our own foibles, and our own weaknesses as well as our strengths and connectedness in the world. The universe encourages us to right-size ourselves and to acknowledge that we are not isolated – not disconnected from nature, the capriciousness of life or each other.

The bottom line in building spiritual resilience is to accept that we are all powerless over something. It does not have to be a chemical or a person – it can simply be life itself. We are all worthy and we all belong on our own priority lists, but spiritual resilience is also paradoxical. It requires us to surrender to win, to realize our smallness to achieve importance and to grieve our losses to find happiness.

Nurturing summed up

This chapter encourages reflection about how well we nurture ourselves. I have learned that I can look back fondly on the young woman I once was, with her smooth skin, shiny hair and skinny body, but I am much happier with the self-nurturing woman I am today.

After spending years placing myself last on my priority list, I now understand that to be a self-actualized person I must work to integrate my mental, physical and spiritual health. I cannot rest on my past achievements. I cannot lament the past, nor wish to hide it away in a closet. I must love my entire self, wholly and unreservedly.

I encourage you to nurture all of you – every wrinkle, every gray hair, every fat cell. Those attributes are evidence that you have lived. They are outward indicators of your experience, your triumphs, your stumbles and the value you have added during your time thus far on Planet Earth.

Nurturing journaling stem:
Self-care assessment

At this point of reinvention, it is critical to examine the habits of self-care we have developed over time. Take a break from reading to complete the Self-Care Assessment which can be downloaded for free at www .reinventioninprogress.com/free-downloads.

FIVE

Values: The Brown Thread

Thus far in our journey of reinvention, we have focused on the past. We have remembered what happened and identified many of the emotions that those events evoked. We have learned about the disorienting effects of divorce, change theory, CPTSD and codependence. In addition, we have learned that through self-advocacy, reducing stress and nurturing ourselves, we can begin to heal old wounds and not only restore ourselves to balance but spin new threads and intertwine them into a new quilt. It is now time to examine our core values.

Knowing what we value is critical to the reinvention process if we want to make good decisions and live authentically. Our values are those essential beliefs we hold most closely to our hearts. Values determine the things we prioritize, motivate our actions, and drive the choices we make about the people, places and things that hold our attention. We can learn a lot about a person by watching how and with whom they choose to spend their time.

My dad built both houses my family lived in while I was growing up. He built our first house before I was born, but he built the second when I was twelve. At that age, I wanted to better understand my father and, because building our house occupied much of his spare time, the only way to be with him was to accompany him to the new home site on evenings and weekends.

Perfectionistic by nature, he would walk the site as I tagged along, talking to himself about some aspect of the building process. He assessed every stage of his work and the craftsmanship of others on the site. Some met his approval, but he considered many of the finished jobs substandard. This would slow the construction timeline as he ripped out previously completed work, only to do it again himself. His nightly mutterings were not usually directed at me, but I absorbed every word he said as if I was taking a masterclass in construction management.

Although my father lacked formal education, he knew his stuff when it came to sound building practices. After the hole for the basement was dug, he worked tirelessly on watering, tamping down and drying the dirt on which the house would rest. He took special care with assembling the forms for the footings and foundation walls.

The day the cement workers poured the concrete, my dad was a meticulous director, supervising the entire process and grinding on the workers to pour properly and work the concrete into every nook and cranny of the forms. When I asked him why he was so hard on those guys, he responded, "You have to start with a strong foundation. Without a solid foundation, the whole house will crack apart and you'll be left with nothing but a pile of rubble."

This made perfect sense to me, and I have applied my observations of that home's construction as metaphors over the years for solving many problems in life. After my divorce, I realized I had to start my new build with a strong foundation. Brown is the color that comes to mind when I think about foundational values and soil is my talisman for the brown thread of my reinvention.

Brown reminds me of the solidity of dirt, trees, rock and other earthly elements that stand the test of time. Our values are like bedrock. They endow us with secure grounding for future planning and a solid surface on which we can plant our feet, establish new balance and begin to grow in alignment with who we really are. Brown characterizes the platform on which our personal reinvention will rest. I added a brown thread to my new fabric because it is a durable color that connotes strength and longevity, just as our values lend power and endurance to our prudent decisions and healthy choices.

Mindsets

We each have a way of looking at life – a perception of the world and our role in it. Carol Dweck (2012), a professor of psychology at Stanford University, refers to mindsets as the belief systems through which human beings make sense of the things that happen around us. Mindsets help us to position ourselves in the world and adapt to challenges.

While each person holds many different mindsets, all mindsets are not equal. Some of us hold mindsets that are "fixed," in which talents are innate and performance is measured by the number of successes or failures experienced. Others develop "growth" mindsets that ready them to learn and grow in every situation they encounter (Dweck, 2012). A person with a fixed mindset will tell you they *are* not good at math, *have never been* good at math and *will never be* good at math. A person with a growth mindset says they have not yet gained their desired proficiency in math but that, through repeated effort, they will eventually master the skill.

People who divorce late in life after long marriages often hold fixed mindsets about relationships but might embrace different mindsets regarding other aspects of their lives. I now recognize that I held firm to a fixed mindset regarding my personal life, but I maintained a growth mindset when it came to my career. I believed it was up to me to make my husband happy, and when I repeatedly failed in that responsibility I gave up and labeled myself a flop. Conversely, when I wanted to get a new job in my profession, I learned all I could about the new role, adopted new behaviors and kept working toward my goal until I achieved it.

Had I been able to nurture a growth mindset in my personal life twenty years ago, I might have left my marriage sooner, determined to continue learning and growing in relationships until I found a partner who could meet my needs and allow me to meet his. Admittedly, it took me a long time to adopt a growth mindset in my personal life, but, now that I have, I am determined to make up for lost time and fully engage in the personal aspects of reinvention.

A long-held fixed mindset blocks our ability to see multiple sides of a story or think creatively about solutions. The more we believe we simply are what we are, the more stuck in the past we become. When someone hears a new approach to a problem and responds with, "I could never do that," or "I refuse to try something new," they are voicing the confirmed beliefs of their fixed mindset.

There is a high price for staying trapped in a fixed mindset. It can keep you from continuing to learn and grow. Over time, one can become attached to belief systems and comfort zones and remain unaware of the powerful role mindsets play in determining thoughts, decisions, words and actions. To maintain a fixed mindset is to choose a self-limiting future.

Understanding fixed and growth mindsets is critical in changing how we interact with the world. When we understand the existence and power of our mindsets, we can change our belief systems about any of our personal attributes (such as intelligence, personality, behaviors, talents or appearance). By shifting our mindset to expect growth and development, we can view every unsuccessful attempt as a mere progress marker on our path toward continued improvement.

When we free ourselves from the tyranny of a fixed mindset, we focus on effort and continued progress toward our own version of what Dweck (2012) defines as personal mastery. Adopting a growth mindset allows us to concentrate on our own arc of improvement. By releasing ourselves from comparisons to other people, we allow them the freedom to be all they can be while we seek to be all we can be. We can make choices and follow our own values, without feeling diminished by the opinions of others or threatened by their successes.

Changing your mindset will take time because old habits die hard, but raising your awareness of your own mindset is half the battle. Realizing that your fixed mindset has limited your growth opens your mind to a host of expanding choices.

As you shift from a fixed to a growth mindset, others will notice. Some will support the changes you are making, but others may dislike the new you that is emerging. They may feel threatened or even resent you for allowing yourself to engage in reinvention. After divorce, people will realize that the circumstances in your life have changed, but they may not appreciate the positive modifications you are making to your mindset.

Because I was married for over forty years, when I told my friends about my divorce some of them could not imagine me making such a decision. After all, I had invested so much time and energy into my relationship, how could I dare to imagine a life beyond the boundaries of the marriage I had so long defended?

Some of those friends abandoned me immediately, and some drifted away over time, but others were willing to listen and appreciate the courage it took to engage in self-examination and reinvention on such a grand scale. By sharing the values I chose as I moved from a fixed to a growth mindset, some of my friends not only began to accept my decision to divorce, but they soon became my greatest supporters. By altering my mindset, I gave them tacit permission to alter their own.

Do my insides match my outsides?

We become motivated to reassess and redesign our core values when we undergo a change that we elected or one that was foisted upon us. When we reach an ending, or we are not happy with the status quo, we are forced to question the values and beliefs we may have held for a lifetime. In the "going through" – the middle of the change process – we recognize that we cannot design a new and colorful life without first reassessing what we believe in now.

When I decided to divorce, I realized that several of my core values would have to change or be abandoned. I acknowledged that my prioritization of loyalty had trapped my thinking and behavior in a fixed mindset for decades. Loyalty had held me in a prison of my own making long past the point where my secondary values of common sense and self-preservation should have propelled me toward freedom.

I am a patient person, and I value optimism about the future, but when I was married my daily life did not support those beliefs. It took me years to see what was happening right before my eyes and accept that the fixed mindset I had long ago created no longer served me. How patient should a person be when waiting for a change that will likely never come? How long should optimism harness us to a cart with no wheels?

When I consciously accepted that my patience and optimism were no longer appropriate to my situation, I became willing to adopt a growth mindset and reexamine my values. The mismatch between my inside beliefs and my outside life became too great to reconcile.

Something had to give, and the remaining threads that held my old life together were slashed beyond repair.

Our values are guideposts that help direct our thinking and let us solve problems and make choices. People are most at peace when their core values match their thoughts, words and actions. Like stacking our joints for good posture, aligning our thoughts and behaviors with our core values helps us achieve emotional balance.

Aligning what we believe inside with how we behave outside makes space in our lives for greater creativity and reinvention. When we invite the sunlight of self-examination and change into our lives, we feed our spirituality and connect ourselves to whomever our growth mindset encourages us to become.

Our core beliefs inform the choices we make, and we can communicate those core beliefs through our words and actions. If the people in our lives know our core values, we are less likely to send mixed messages, and we can often sidestep future regrets, embarrassment and even shame.

The values we hold dear develop as we combine our inner nature and newly formed growth mindset with our experiences – our culture, family background, religious training, education, and what we read and learn – over time. As children, our values often reflect those of our families of origin. During our teen years, the friends with whom we share laughter, tears and secrets frequently influence the values we develop. Our adult values solidify with the work we do, the spouse we may choose, the in-laws they bring and any children we may or may not elect to have.

As we live longer and experience more, our core values may change completely, or their order of importance may shift, so completing a values clarification exercise after age fifty is essential as we set new goals and life purposes. Knowing your own values gives you a leg up in leading an authentically colorful life. Understanding your core beliefs can assist you in mitigating internal and external conflicts. You might find yourself associating with people who do not share your values but knowing what you believe can help you respectfully articulate your point of view without apology or pretense. You can only achieve authenticity by showing your true colors to the world.

Reinventing your mindset

At this point in the process of reinvention, it is time to adopt a growth mindset that can accommodate the core values that fit you now. Think of your values as the foundation you will lay for your reinvented physical, mental and spiritual home. A strong foundation supports not only the load of the building itself but the weight of any elements you may add in the future: new people, experiences, hobbies or activities.

Renewed values provide foundational strength to build a new shelter for your mind, body and spirit. The strength of the convictions that support your choices must be the basis for the new you. A strong set of new values or recommitting to values you have held for a lifetime will keep you grounded even if your commitment to your decisions may waver. With a sturdy foundation, you will be able to carry whatever your load demands of you on any given day and make a positive impact on situations and people around you.

Placing your renewed values at the center of your growth mindset will allow you more freedom to try new things, take risks and say "yes" to the opportunities that will come your way. The refreshed energy you apply to living, the reinvented spring in your step and the new colors that shine from you will undoubtedly bring you novel opportunities for connection, participation and growth. You want to be prepared to say "yes" when it suits you, secure in the knowledge that you have done the work to create a strong sense of self and a presence in the world that communicates who you are and what you want.

Keep in mind that it takes courage to examine your values and establish new guiding principles. It can be unsettling to challenge lifelong beliefs and worn-out ideologies, but it is worth the struggle. Go forward boldly into a healthy growth mindset. You may be pleasantly surprised by what you learn about yourself.

Prune your garden

A renewed commitment to your values will infuse new energy into your reinvention process. However, as you modernize your values, you will likewise need to prune your garden to make space for new thoughts, opportunities, people and things. Just as cleaning out your closet makes room for new clothes, pruning away old memories, scarred-over injuries and worn-out belief systems reduces mental, emotional and spiritual clutter.

We may also need to prune certain people from our lives. Self-actualized women who operate with growth mindsets can stand on their own two feet. We are continuously seeking to learn and grow, but we do not need others to make us whole. Over our lives, we have built relationships with many people. Some of those relationships have lasted a lifetime and some have only lasted a day, a week, a few months or years. While every relationship has taught us something, we don't need to carry them all into our futures. You have the power to preserve any relationship you choose to keep, but you can best serve your mental, physical and spiritual wellbeing by nurturing only those people who accept you as you are today, appreciate you for the gifts you bring and foster your journey of reinvention.

For me to move forward into a healthy and colorful outlook, I needed to adopt a new habit of examining the people and things in my life to determine for myself if they still fit. This process can be heartbreaking and financially challenging. When I left my marital home, I walked away from many things I had grown accustomed to. However, once free of the weight of these tired possessions, I felt lighter and oddly liberated. I chose to set up my new home in a minimalist fashion and discovered that less is indeed more.

By physically living lighter, I have opened many doors for new opportunities. I am now able to travel, to move somewhere else if I choose, to invite new people into my life, and to continue growing and learning. I can choose to work or not. I can move in whatever direction I desire. I can work on my health, buy whatever I want within my budget, and make my own decisions about where and with whom I spend my time.

By freeing myself of the detritus that bogged me down for decades, I cleared a path to move forward. Just as I am no longer a prisoner to the stuff I used to own, I am no longer beholden to old attitudes, behaviors, and beliefs about myself and other people. I have found a new freedom and, though I mourned the loss of some of those things, I discovered that I am much happier when I carry less baggage.

Some 12-Step programs such as Al-Anon refer to this pruning process as "detachment with love" (Al-Anon Family Groups, 2008, p. 85). This concept describes letting go without rancor. By detaching with love and placing the richness of my history in the past, I can reflect with gentleness while moving forward with courage. I can release my death grip on people, places and things, knowing that they are safely held in my long-term memory. I can move forward without allowing them to negatively impact my present.

I won't lie: Letting go can be frightening, particularly if you are like me and you've flown most of your life without a safety net. You might ask yourself, "If I let go of this, what will replace it?" but by asking this question, you are readying yourself for the next step in the reinvention process.

Finding your answer to, "What will replace what I've lost?" is your new sacred work. You are preparing to create an innovative vision of what life might look like when you let go of things, memories and people that no longer hold promise, no longer meet your needs and no longer serve the core values you have identified for yourself. You are lightening your physical and emotional load, and you are gaining a willingness to enter a whole new world of aspirations.

Valuing yourself

Establishing a strong set of core values is a critical step in reinvention, but that alone is not enough; we must also explicitly value ourselves. We live by our values, but if we fail to value ourselves we are unlikely to adhere to our guiding principles. Using a growth mindset to help you determine who you are now and what you value is more than building self-esteem. It is the acceptance and appreciation of the one-of-a-kind human being you are.

Valuing yourself does not rely on relationships with other people. At the moment of your birth, you were a gift to this world, and as you have moved through your life you have brought with you a unique set of feelings, talents, faults, beauties and perceptions. There has never been another you and, after you're gone, there will never be another you.

Valuing yourself, just as you are, does not mean you do not have work to do. It simply means that, by virtue of your uniqueness, you have intrinsic value. We can all improve ourselves but accepting that we have value just because we exist will lead to greater self-awareness, self-care and self-improvement. Knowing and valuing who we are at our core will contribute to our resilience – perhaps like nothing else can.

To get in touch with our self-worth, we must release ourselves from comparison to others. When we compare our own "insides" (our feelings, doubts, worries and fears) to other people's "outsides" (social media posts, photographs, achievements, relationships and appearance) we set ourselves up for self-criticism and uncertainty. This is the essence of a fixed mindset. It is easy to feel "less than" when we engage in comparison to others.

Valuing ourselves requires remembering that, in this age of social media, we are bombarded by words and images of what other people would like us to see as their truth. On social media platforms, it often appears as if everyone else is doing better than we are. Their food looks better than what we eat. They have more fun on vacation. Their bodies are in better shape. Their clothes are more stylish.

I am certainly not advocating that we disengage from these platforms, which can be useful for information sharing. I am instead suggesting that we limit the importance of what we find there and consistently remind ourselves that people generally don't post stories, pictures or videos of themselves doing the hard work of reinvention.

It is difficult to take a picture of a growth mindset. People could post pictures of themselves trying new things, failing and trying again, but we rarely encounter this on social media sites. We typically do not see other people's pain, their frustration or their moments of insecurity. To allow self-love into our lives, comparisons between ourselves and curated images of other people must go.

Valuing ourselves demands that we fully accept our weaknesses. To have faults is to be human, and it is only by accepting our own humanity that we can grow. When we use our growth mindsets, we invest time in self-improvement, but wholly valuing ourselves means that we do not beat ourselves up about who and what we presently are. We work to be the best that we can be while accepting that we will always be somewhat flawed. That's what makes us interesting!

By being honest with ourselves about our drawbacks, we can empathize with others as they, too, experience the entirety of the human condition. We can include others in our circle of compassion, forgiving more easily and resisting the urge to take offense. We can give proper weight and importance to our qualities and our experiences.

Why is it so important to value oneself? When we value ourselves and establish our core inner values, we take back our own personal power. Rather than being doormats for others, we can set boundaries, communicate them and stick to them. We can afford to be flexible when appropriate, yet absolutist when the values closest to our core are challenged. We do not bow down or grovel to anyone. We walk with purpose as powerful individuals in a world that sometimes tries to take us down. To value oneself is the greatest gift anyone can give to themselves and to the world.

Values journaling stem: Values clarification worksheet

As you delve deeper into your reinvention, a growth mindset and clarified values will help you redefine and honor your priorities as you develop into a colorful new you.

One way to clarify your beliefs and principles is to examine a list of values and determine which ones apply to you now. Read the Values Clarification Worksheet www.reinventioninprogress.com/free-downloads and think about which values most closely align with the person you want to become. Which values will help you be true to yourself now and expand your life to include the effort, lessons and self-development that emerge from a growth mindset?

SIX
Envisioning:
The Yellow Thread

You have made significant headway in creating a strong foundation for the colorful new life you want to live – now it is time to have some fun! Envisioning what you want out of this stage in your life is an imaginative practice and, with your memories secure, your emotions regulated, your self-knowledge in hand, your tools for self-nurturing at the ready and your values identified, you are prepared to put your collection of new skills to work. You are primed to add another thread to the new fabric of your life: envisioning the future you.

After my divorce was resolved, I used my settlement money to purchase a newly built home. As with all new houses, the inside was complete, but the landscaping was not done. I spent the end of my first summer there putting in the basics; grass, trees, bushes and rocks. Soon after that work was finished, the weather turned cold and the Colorado winter was upon me.

The fall and winter of 2019–2020 seemed endless. Not only did we have a stormy winter, but the isolation that accompanied the COVID-19 quarantine made the season feel interminable. However, much to my delight, the beginning of May finally brought warmer temperatures and I decided to add a bit of floral color to my garden.

In the past, I had not been particularly choosy about which flowers I planted outside. Because my old house was in the foothills of the Rocky Mountains, my main consideration there had been to choose plants that were not appealing to hungry deer and elk. But this year was different. I chose flowers based on the colors that I thought would lift my mood and encourage hope.

To help me decide on a central color for my new flower beds, I returned to my RCAC. In many cultures, yellow is the color of optimism, joy and vitality, so I chose it to inspire my process of envisioning a brilliant new future. Yellow invigorates my imagination and gives me permission to play with new ideas about what my best life might look like. Yellow is sunny and warm and lights up my dreams for the future. It opens my mental, emotional and spiritual windows.

I settled on the sunflower as the lead plant for my garden and an outdoor talisman for my process of envisioning. Supported by strong stalks and deep roots, sunflowers flourish throughout the summer and fall. They explode with bright star blossoms and thrive even in the strong sunlight and dry conditions of Colorado. Sunflowers inspired me to weave a bright yellow thread into the cloth of my new life. Yellow would help me create a new vision for my future.

The epicenter of your sacred work

Envisioning is more than just creating a vision statement for yourself. It is not a sudden realization that wakes you up in the middle of the night and then sinks back into the recesses of your subconscious by morning. It is not an "aha" moment that changes the trajectory of your life. Envisioning is a longer and deeper process that requires time and reflection. It is more sustainable than sudden flashes of brilliance.

Envisioning is the epicenter of your sacred work from this moment forward. Embrace who you are at your core and what is best for you. You are already wise, even if you do not yet realize it. Sit in the quiet, close your eyes, and imagine who and what you could be without any artificial limitations.

Remember, you are not creating someone else's dream *for* you, nor are you adopting someone else's expectations *of* you. This vision is yours, and yours alone. You are beholden to no one, so if you begin to hear old criticisms or voices of negativity in your head during this process, simply soften those thoughts and imagine yourself gently placing them on a small table that sits behind you, just out of your field of inner vision. Envisioning does not require you to fight with or against any competing idea or memory. It is a placid process in which old pain is simply moved away to make room for the bright color and peace of today.

Envisioning frees you to dream any dream you want for yourself. Although of course you are grounded in reality, when you envision, you are not limited by time or space. To envision is to release the power of your imagination. It prevails over knowledge because it honors the energy beings that we are. Flesh and blood are temporal, but energy is eternal.

As you learn to practice envisioning, you will begin to make your imagined future real. Through envisioning, you allow yourself to let go of all restricting factors, other people's attitudes, other people's expectations, and your own self-limiting points of view about money, time, power and possibilities. Free envisioning allows you to think only of abundance and let go of the constraints of lack.

Envisioning is not trapped in the solidity of the past, nor does it define you for eternity; it allows you to establish a new habit of thinking that empowers your dreams and welcomes potential and fluidity. Envisioning is also the point at which you push your thinking outside the margins of the head field and lean into the energy-expanding opportunities generated in the heart field.

Envisioning from the heart allows you to release pain that was once embodied in old memories and embrace the joy that awaits you in a future not yet real. By envisioning a fresh start, you begin to put old emotional attachments into perspective and release them to the powers of the cosmos, or to the God of your understanding, or incorporate them within whatever spiritual foundation you have built for yourself thus far.

You are filled with self-knowledge, but what has happened to you or been done to you in the past does not confine you. You are now free to employ your refreshed values, your renewed nurturing techniques and your ability to dream big. By allowing your heart, your imagination and your spiritual connection to drive your future, you will surpass any expectations you ever held for yourself. When we envision what could be, there are no boundaries, no regulators, no rules for creating your own vision for you.

For some, envisioning a powerful future can be difficult to start, particularly if you have not completed the exercises from my website that prepare you for this process. Wild, ill-equipped and unaware envisioning can feel rudderless and frightening; but, if you know yourself and you give yourself permission to reengage with the child you once were, envisioning is exciting, enjoyable, playful and fun.

I often played imaginative games with my children, and still do with my grandchildren, but when I first tried to do so on my own, for myself, I felt a little silly. I worried that, as an adult, I had spent so much time in a grown-up world fraught with work, duty, worry and obligations, I would not be able to reconnect with my child self. To engage in the playfulness of envisioning, I had to let go of my fixed mindset that informed me that adults are too old to play. Exploring, imagining, discovering – playing – is a human endeavor, meant for us at every age. Just as I had watched others to learn about self-care, I now observed my grandchildren to relearn how to engage in imaginative play.

Children at play don't see limits or barriers to their own creations. If something is not yet there in reality, they simply fill in the blank and move on. They are not worried about how to make something happen. They simply design an imaginative world and happily live there until they choose to change the scene. Naturally, as an adult, I understood that just making up a wished-for reality was not going to bring about real change, but I needed to free up the cogs of my imagination to allow myself to envision what I could prepare to make real in my future. When I decided to change my fixed mindset about play to a growth mindset, I knew that with practice, I could bridge the gap between my current reality and the future I wanted to create.

Envisioning is The New Beginning (Bridges, 1991) – it's when you push the reset button on your life. Use the tools you have gathered thus far and shift your mindset to free your imagination to start creating a flexible plan for today and for all the tomorrows yet to come.

A free ride into the future

Close your eyes, relax and breathe deeply for a few minutes. Begin to imagine yourself five, ten or twenty years from now. Release any fears you may be harboring about your future self and summon only positive thoughts of the reinvented woman you will become.

The woman you see in your future has long ago stepped through the rip in her fabric. She has conquered her demons and is living the bountiful life you are dreaming of today. What does she look like? Where is she living? What colors and textures make up the fabric of her life now? Go willingly as she invites you on a tour of her home and her surroundings. Observe the sights, sounds and smells. What clues can you pick up about how she spends her time and with whom?

This woman is the true you, the essence of your inner calm and tranquility. If she were to speak to you, what would she say? Listen to her soothing voice. What advice does she give you as you are becoming her? Perhaps she will remind you of the goodness within your spirit, or she may encourage you to become more open to self-acceptance and love. Does she share any thoughts about how she let go of pain, resentment or fear? What brings her joy and what does her laughter sound like?

If she offers you a gift, accept it gracefully. What did she give you and why do you think she chose that object? What meaning do you attach to the woman you will become and the gifts she has to offer?

Embrace her before you return to the present, knowing that she is your goal, your goddess, your wisdom. She is you and you are her. You can trust her to lead you to the light that will guide your envisioning process. She will show you the next right step, the next right move toward your reinvented future. She is your reassurance that you are on the right path toward a life filled with hope and a colorful outlook.

Learn more about my visit with my future self by visiting my website at www.reinventioninprogress .com/blog.

Planning for your reinvented future

As you return from your visit with your future self, give some thought to the aspects of her life that intrigued you. Take some time to journal about the woman you met. What was present in her life that you do not yet have? What has she accomplished in the time that stands between where you are today and where she is? Think about the steps she took to attain her appearance, her home, her sense of inner peace. What elements did she add to her life and what components did she prune from her garden to become the woman she is?

The woman you saw in your future vision holds the specifics of the plan you will develop for your reinvention. When we envision a better future for ourselves, we must set clear intentions about where we want to go and be willing to do the emotional and physical foot work to ensure we get there. What guidance did you acquire from your future self about how to set specific goals for your next right step? Record your initial thoughts in your journal. You will use them as you begin to weave a new cloth for your future.

It is critical at this stage that you refuse to be stymied by fear. Dig deep to confront limitations that may have frightened you earlier in life and just go for it. Consider how the woman you will become overcame her fear. I was terrified to release my past self, but I knew that if I wanted to finish my life in an authentic manner, I had to let go of old ways of doing and thinking, and step out into my own life. Simply put, I had to face my fear or stay stuck.

Years of training and life experience had given me sound judgement and the skills to reinvent myself. I had developed enough wisdom to recognize what I could and could not change, so I focused my planning on those things I could reasonably affect. While sound planning and hard work do not always produce the result we expect, they do always create an altered outcome. My job was to make the plan and do the foot work, then leave the results of my efforts up to my Higher Power.

Once I reached the jumping-off point, I was still afraid, but I took the leap anyway, trusting that my years of preparation had given me the ability to make wise choices. Leaving seemed to go against every instinct I had to protect my emotional and financial resources, but after I visited with my future self, I realized that I would never arrive at her unless I fully invested in the truer purpose she demonstrated. To reach that happier version of myself, I had to release my death grip on the past.

By moving through the steps of reinvention, honestly remembering, feeling my emotions, understanding how and why I made choices, learning how to nurture myself and reclarifying my values, I envisioned the future I am living now. Today, I take full responsibility for my own happiness. Through envisioning, I empowered my hopes and by intentionally fostering a growth mindset, I made real a life I once could only dream about. While my future self gave me direction on where to go, my current self gave me permission to play with ideas, dream big and continue to evolve over time.

If you have always kindled the spark of a dream that your experience and common sense tell you might still be attainable, you may want to include it in your refreshed vision for your future. I went to graduate school with a woman who started our program at fifty-seven years of age. She was the oldest person in our class, and I know she held some trepidation about undertaking such an arduous journey at her age.

When she introduced herself to our cohort, she proudly announced her intention to graduate and work with students with disabilities. Although the program would take three years to complete, she was undaunted by the fact that she would be nearly sixty when we finished. After all, she would turn sixty in three years, with or without an advanced degree. Her growth mindset demanded that she press forward into a reinvented future.

This woman became one of my best friends in the program and served for many years thereafter as my mentor and sounding board. Had she held on to a fixed mindset and based her choice about returning to school solely on her age, we would never have met, and my little corner of the world would have been poorer without the benefit of her experience, judgement and wisdom. By trusting her skills, believing in her dream of reinvention, planning for her future and doing the hard work required to get there, my friend spent the remainder of her career enriching the lives of students and colleagues alike. She set the intention, did the foot work and trusted that the outcome would take care of itself.

Learning from those who have "been there, done that"

As you continue to ruminate about your experience with your future self, ask yourself this: "How did she become so happy?" Common collective wisdom suggests that we are a culture obsessed with youth and that young people have a corner on the happiness market. Through the lens of nostalgia, we recollect our own youthful days and often make the mistake of assuming that our best and happiest days are behind us. As you continue to sew a new garment in which to clothe your future self, I invite you to consider another possibility.

The world likes to place people into categories, and delineate who should be doing what, based on stereotypes. Societal labels, along with our own fixed mindsets, can sometimes place artificial limitations on the envisioning process. People who are over fifty are often not seen. At a certain age, the world tends to write people off. It either regards us as the aged, a part of the population who creates problems and no longer contributes to solutions, or we simply become invisible. As a society, we waste so much living knowledge by dismissing our oldest citizens.

Karl Pillemer, head of the Cornell Legacy Project, agrees. In his 2011 book, *30 Lessons for Living: Tried and true advice from the wisest Americans,* Pillemer asserts that, though we seek self-help books and advice from many different sources, we often ignore the most obvious gold mine for direction on not only surviving hard times but also transforming tough experiences into our moments of greatest growth. By tapping into the knowledge, experience and common sense of the oldest among us, we can easily find simple solutions to what we perceive as our greatest challenges.

Pillemer and his associates interviewed 1,000 "experts" (Americans over the age of sixty-five) to extract their best advice on living and loving. The number-one takeaway was that older people tend to view happiness as a choice. Circumstances often have less influence on happiness than attitude. It could be said that survivors in life "act as if" they are happy – and, by doing so, experience happiness.

Our society today is dominated by advertisements, images, TV shows, websites and social media platforms that try to convince us that happiness is "out there." If you buy this car, you'll have a great Christmas. If you lose weight, you'll be loveable. If you take this perfect vacation, you'll be relaxed.

However, the oldest Americans reveal that achieving peace, health and happiness is an inside job. It has little to do with where you live, which car you drive or how much money you make. While many of us have discovered this for ourselves along the way, it's great to know that the oldest among us validate our suspicions. Since we are already vested with the power of choice, why not *choose* to be happy. Envision a happier future, then do the foot work to make it so.

Please recognize that the time to make that choice is right now, not five or ten years from now. The time to reinvent is today. For many of us, much of our time allotment on Earth is in the rearview mirror – so, if not now, when? Start envisioning today how you want to spend your tomorrows. We will discuss time in greater detail in Chapter 8, but for now, let's focus on the idea that there is no more time to waste on things like worry, fear, regret, anger, resentment, hurt or anything we cannot change about the past. These are merely distractions from the work at hand and they block our ability to creatively envision a reinvented future for ourselves.

Instead, let us envision those things we can affect. Where do we want to spend our time and with whom? What resources do we have to work with as we plan for our colorful future? To whom can we give our gifts of knowledge, experience and wisdom? How can we help others or take steps to pull someone out of the jaws of impending disaster by sharing our ability to solve problems and survive difficulties?

Mother Teresa once said, "The greatest disease in the West today is not TB or leprosy; it is being unwanted, unloved and uncared for" (1995). Perhaps part of your vision for your future will be to solidify your legacy of love. Maybe your vision will simply be to take good care of yourself. It is your vision and only you can determine its color and design.

Envisioning is an inside job

For now, speak only to yourself about your envisioning process. You do not owe anyone an explanation about what you are doing to feed your future or why you are doing it. Once you have put your newly envisioned plan into action, people may wonder what is different about you. They may ask why you look younger or refreshed. They may not be sure what you've been up to, but they will likely observe that you look like a new person.

Down the road, when folks observe that you appear restored, you may casually mention that you've been doing some work on your inner self. Keep in mind that your journey of reinvention is between your own head and heart. You are not required to share anything about the work you have done. At some point, you may elect to share everything about your progress, but whether you share it or not, your ascendance to a new you is your own expedition. You alone are in the driver's seat of your envisioning work and reinvention process.

You are on a personal journey, and your goal is to design a future that works for you. Other people may have their opinions, but yours is the only one that counts right now.

Envisioning journaling stems

Stem 1: Sharing your gifts

The process of envisioning our future requires us to consider that everyone has talents and skills to share. Think about what you possess that might help others. We can all name a gifted athlete, a talented singer or an inspiring orator, but what abilities do you bring to the table of life?

Maybe you are mechanically skilled or able to think analytically or abstractly. Perhaps you have artistic talent or the gift of gab. Maybe you are empathetic and compassionate or promote humor wherever you go. Whatever your talent, it can improve your quality of life when you share it with others. Consider your personal gifts and, in your journal, list your assets. What do you have to offer to the world and how might you use your gifts as you add color to your reinvented future?

Stem 2: Creating your plan

Use the journal entries you created after your visit with your future self to begin to design a new plan for living. Where do you want to reside five or ten years from now? Will you live alone, or will there be another love in your life? What role will your family and friends play? What will you need to prune from your garden to make your plan for living possible?

In addition, how will you free your imagination to play with new ideas for your future? Changing from a fixed mindset to a growth mindset is a choice, but completing the shift takes time and practice. Be sure to include graduated steps to help you accomplish this goal in your plan.

You will find a Planning Guide for Reinvention to help you with this process at www.reinventioninprogress .com/free-downloads.

SEVEN
Networking:
The Orange Thread

We are all social beings. From the moment we are born, we depend on others for our very survival. As we grow, we become interdependent with the whole of society. Since none of us can be good at everything, we need the skills and gifts of other human beings to help us maintain our health, become educated, move from place to place, put food on our tables, and live full and rewarding lives.

There are significant health implications when we continue old habits of placing others' needs before our own, and this can be a hard habit to break. However, despite the painful events in our past, we are the lucky ones. We have lived long enough to begin to see the value we bring to the world. By finding ways to say "yes" to the expansion of our network, we are sharing our wisdom with our fellows as well as benefiting from the wisdom of others.

People with strong social connection tend to live longer and often report feeling a desire to care for themselves and others. Our social connections give us positive attitudes and feelings of hope and wellbeing. The US Office of Disease Prevention and Health Promotion asserts that social cohesion, access to social services like education and health care, economic stability and healthy environmental conditions are critical to maintaining good physical and emotional health (Lansky, 2020).

The need for social connection is part of the human condition. Having a sense of belonging is as or more important to overall health as weight management, avoiding self-destructive behaviors such as smoking and other forms of substance abuse, and self-care behaviors that improve our cardiovascular health and reduce our blood pressure (Lansky, 2020). Therefore, connection may not only improve your life – it may extend it.

Quirks of connection

When I became the principal of a large neighborhood high school, I noticed that it was becoming increasingly more difficult to read my notes during all-school pep rallies or while speaking to parents on back-to-school night. I visited my eye doctor, who prescribed magnifying glasses when reading print up close. When I went shopping for reading glasses, I discovered there were hundreds of colors to choose from, and my addiction to reading glasses that matched my clothes was born.

I had a favorite suit at the time. It was made of a shimmery russet orange fabric and fit like a glove. Naturally, I needed a pair of glasses to go with it, and after some searching I found one that was the exact color of my suit. My matching orange glasses became conversation starters, even with the hardest-to-reach students, and I began to realize how easy it was to break down barriers between people just by bringing a little quirky humanity into any relationship.

This recollection came to mind and orange became my natural color choice for building relationships in my reinvented life. I vividly remember how I felt when I wore my orange suit and matching glasses, and how they seemed to attract other people. Thus, as orange became my thread color for networking, my old pair of orange glasses became my talisman.

Orange is a friendly and lively color. It pops with energy and vitality and puts a spring in my step. Orange makes me feel more approachable and seems to invite conversation. It elevates my mood and encourages me to try new things and look for ways to say "yes" to opportunities that come my way.

When I see orange in my mind's eye, I enjoy a better level of mental, physical and spiritual health. Orange is warm and allows me to be open-minded. It frees me to recognize and accept the kindness and love I receive from other people. Orange takes me to unexplored regions of my imagination and permits me to run wild, be creative and infuse freshness into my thinking.

In many cultures around the world, orange is the color of fun and adventure. As I began to restore old relationships and generate new ones, orange encouraged me to approach networking armed with the knowledge of who I was and the hope of who I wanted to attract into my new life.

To select your color of association for expanding your social network, you may choose to consult the RCAC found on my website at www.reinventioninprogress .com/free-downloads. Choose the color that will best support your personal excursion into quirky new ways to connect.

Why is networking vital?

People are living longer as we progress through the twenty-first century. Many older adults find themselves sandwiched between the generations of their children and their elderly parents. The competing demands of both worlds can leave us feeling caught between the two, but not fitting into either.

In this situation, the first thing we usually disregard is our own welfare. When we try to manage our own health and relationship needs in addition to the needs of others, we can easily fall short of expectations for ourselves as well as for our older and younger loved ones.

A divorce later in life can add one more layer of complication to our already busy lives. Divorce brings weighty and often disturbing changes to the social network that used to sustain us. Who keeps the friends that were made during the marriage? Do we lose contact with any of our in-laws? Who gets to stay in familiar surroundings among neighbors, shop owners and service providers – those people who may be ancillary to our network but stabilize us during times of seismic change?

Divorce also brings changes in the regular interactions you enjoyed while participating in activities as half of a couple. Which of you gets to stay on the bowling league or in the bridge group? Who gets to continue playing golf with the same old crowd? Who keeps the spot on the trivia team that competes at the local watering hole? Considering the upheaval that divorce brings to our daily social life, our reinvention must include a reawakening and a redesign of our social network.

As we age, we lose people along the way. People die, or move away, or – in the case of divorce – elect to not associate with us anymore, yet social connection is central to our emotional wellbeing. The world can be an unhealthy place for a person who is isolated. This fact became evident during the COVID-19 pandemic when people of all ages were isolated from each other and found themselves facing loneliness, worry, depression and/or despair.

It is harder to accomplish tasks by yourself – and it's less fun. Our interactions with others enhance our self-esteem. Being of service to others can provide us with a reason to go on. Getting up in the morning can seem pointless if you have nowhere to go, nothing to do and no one to do it with.

Even our daily interactions with people we do not like add spice to the stories we tell our friends. While I don't advocate harmful gossip, we all talk about each other, and if you never do anything and never see anyone you have nothing to share in these harmless conversations.

In addition to having fun with other people, we learn from each other. Human beings are social animals, and we learn how to do many things from observing and interacting with other people. We need others to reflect back to us our value, love, comfort, intelligence and achievement. Without their input, it is difficult – if not impossible – to develop healthy personality traits, interests, activities and relationships.

My social network

When I was divorcing and new to living alone, I initially succumbed to an urge to shut my front door, close my blinds, silence my phone and pretend to no longer exist. There was no one I wanted to talk to, no one I wanted to confide in. I had no desire to go anywhere or do anything. I did not want to meet my new neighbors. I did not want to entertain, or play cards, or socialize at all. All I wanted to do was isolate myself, lick my wounds and plan for my last remaining years of solitude. My world was indeed gray, and it seemed that rejection from one person had inspired me to recoil from society at large.

When I first moved into my new place, it felt empty and echoed with settling house noises and unpacked boxes. It was devoid of any joy or laughter or happy memories. It held no memories at all. My home was but a vessel that housed me. It protected me from the wind and rain, but it did not give me comfort.

Thankfully, there were people in my life who did not let me follow my instinct to isolate. Shortly after I moved into my new home, an old friend called and invited herself to spend a week with me. Although I was happy to see her, I would not have invited her to visit at such an inopportune time. After all, how could I wallow in my misery with her around?

Despite my misgivings, that visit began to crack the wall of glass I was building between me and the rest of the world. When my friend arrived for her week-long stay, she introduced love into my new home. Together, during that week of tears and laughter she and I created new memories and gave my post-divorce life a start. When she left, I knew those memories would carry me into my future.

I learned from my friend's visit that to create a new life I would have to change some of my old habits and find ways to say "yes" to opportunities. I needed courage to put myself out there to meet new people and have new experiences. I would have to learn to ask for advice regarding my home, my car, my yard. I would need self-discipline to establish a healthy routine and not allow depression to make me sleep all day or stay up all night. I would have to motivate myself to keep busy, to keep moving forward.

After my first friend left, a second showed up for another week-long visit. With her, I made more memories and moved further away from the past. After she left, my first friend returned, again without an invitation. She merely called to tell me which day she would arrive.

These wonderful women gave me no choice about whether to host them in my house. They just showed up to listen, to advise, to remind me I was loved, to relax, to watch TV, to provide company, and to help me continue to put one foot in front of the other. Between them, these two friends – sisters of support – gave me something to look forward to, something to live for over the first few months following my divorce. With each visit, my friends left behind fresh and pain-free memories, and they gave me tacit approval to start living again.

As time passed, I met a few neighbors, and I became friendly with some women I met in a writers' group I joined. At the suggestion of one of my new neighbors, I attended a Meetup where I met women and men, and it dawned on me that I might have something to offer to more people than just the narrow circle of friends I had had during my marriage.

Hold on to your hat, but during this time I also began to date! The men I went out with treated me with such dignity and respect, I will hold a special place in my heart for each of them for the rest of my life. They reminded me of my femininity, my sense of humor, my enjoyment of simple pleasures, my love for live music, and my ability to go out for dinner or a movie with someone caring and kind. They did not think there was anything wrong, old or boring about me. Who knew?

During the months following my divorce, I also started using Zoom and other online meeting applications, where I met more interesting people. When the COVID-19 shutdown occurred, I continued to build friendships online. Although, like everyone, I was physically isolated in my house, I remained able to sustain my social network through online coffees, book clubs, writing seminars and supportive conversations. Some of the people I met online became friends in real life, and those relationships evolved organically over time.

Although the pandemic caused death, economic hardship and suffering on a huge scale around the globe, it also created reasons for people to rekindle old friendships. During this time, I reconnected with the first friend I had in life, a woman who I met at the age of four in kindergarten class. I also reconnected with old friends from thirty-five years of work and added them to my growing social network.

Several acquaintances also re-entered my universe during the months after my divorce. Most of these people were professionals with whom I had maintained a working relationship for decades. My accountant, my massage therapist, my hair stylist, my dog sitter and my yoga teacher all stepped forward, and I realized that they had become more than acquaintances – they had become friends.

As one of these "acquaintance-friends" said at the end of a phone call, "Remember, you are our friend, and we are here for you. Let us know how we can help," I realized at that moment that he and his wife were previously unidentified members of my social network. I was stunned at the level of support, caring and concern I received from people in this category.

These were folks I had been friendly with for a long time, yet I had not known how much they cared about me until my divorce.

I was often astounded and humbled by the love and support I received from almost everyone I met, and, as each person emerged as a friend, I added them to my forward-facing social network. It was as if the universe, the cosmos or my Higher Power was working in my life and doing for me what I could never have done for myself. My network was aiding in my healing and weaving me into a tapestry of love. I was living a rich and reinvented life with new and old friends wrapping themselves around me like a warm blanket. Even in winter, the sun was shining again, and color was re-emerging from the shadows.

Reinvigorating your network

Given where you are in your reinvention process, and knowing the many benefits of social connections, what can you do to create or expand your own social network?

The following activities might capture your interest and allow you to maximize your social connectedness:

1. If color appeals to you, think and journal about what color you would associate with networking. Remember, mine is orange, but yours may be

different. Choose your color and identify why it screams social connection for you.

2. Reach out to neighbors, friends, family, coworkers and others. Tell them about your divorce and your new social need to connect. You do not have to go into detail about your past but give people enough information to understand your changed circumstance. You may be surprised by how willing your listeners are to assist you as you make the transition from half of a couple to a single.

3. Open yourself to accepting help. You may be better at this than I am, but this is no time to be prideful. Remember: our task in creating a new network is finding ways to say "yes" to opportunities for connections. This means we say "yes" to invitations, "yes" to offers of assistance, "yes" to meeting new people, and "yes" to visits with friends.

4. If you are not computer literate, sign up for a course to improve your skills. Learn how to use the Internet and the digital tools that can help you connect with others online. You may not immediately feel safe enough to meet people face to face, but anything is possible online if you practice safe Internet rules: never share your private information such as your Social Security or government identification number, your banking information, your address, or your phone number.

5. If you don't already have one, get an email address. Consider setting up an Instagram or a Twitter account. You may want to join LinkedIn or Meetup, enroll in an online class or give online support groups a try. 12 Step and other counseling groups offer self-development programs to people of all ages.

6. Investigate new hobbies. Learn to knit or dance. Sign up for classes or Meetups where you will find others who share your passions and hobbies.

7. Exercise. Get outside. Take a walk, do yoga, practice mindfulness – participate in activities that will take you out of your head and help you develop an interest in others.

8. Return to school or take a college course. Try learning about something you have never studied before. You may be surprised at how fun it is to challenge yourself to learn a new skill. The welcome you receive from your younger classmates may also surprise you. Stretch your mind and expand your thinking.

9. Be brave. Ask other people to do things and accept invitations when an activity piques your interest. A few months after my divorce, a woman I met asked if I wanted to attend a line dancing class with her. I thought to myself, "Line dancing? I've never even considered trying it, but who knows? It might be fun." Did I adopt it as a hobby? No, but I had fun that evening, and at

least I now know that line dancing is probably not going to be part of my reinvention plan.

10. If you attended services at a place of worship in the past but have not been going lately, think about returning. If you have never been, think about trying it. While a place of worship is only one of the many avenues people use to acquire spiritual connection, they are filled with people who are, like you, seeking spiritual growth, and you may meet your next best friend there.

11. Get politically active. We are all aware that the world today is divided among various polarizing viewpoints. If that condition bothers you, or if you affiliate with one of those viewpoints, consider joining a political campaign. If you do not affiliate with a political action group, find organizations that are interested in bridging the gap. They are always looking for help.

12. Volunteer. Use your expertise and your spirit of service to help someone else. Helping others is another way to get out of your head and focus your attention elsewhere. You might enjoy:

- Serving on an advisory board

- Working for a hospital or museum

- Tutoring college students

- Substitute teaching

- Mentoring young people who are just starting out

- Volunteering in animal welfare or social service organizations

13. Get to know your neighbors. You don't have to be a busybody or the neighborhood gossip, but introduce yourself to people you may have seen thousands of times while leaving or returning home. Get to know the people who live around you.

14. Date. Many of us who find ourselves alone later in life wall ourselves off from the prospect of dating. We worry about the shape of our bodies, our emotional baggage, what our kids and other family members will think, whether we have forgotten how to interact with the gender to which we are attracted, and whether we are too old to start again. If you are lonely or wish to keep sex and intimacy in your life, be brave! Let your freak flag fly and learn to flirt again. Buy some new clothes, take dance lessons, reinvigorate your sensual side with opportunities to meet new people who are also interested in dating. You might surprise yourself. I know I did. Who knew after all these years that men could find me interesting – even sexy?

15. Once you have established a network, be active in it. Fill your calendar as much or as little as you choose, but maintain the relationships you

have worked hard to build for the sake of your emotional, physical and spiritual health.

Mr. F.'s adventure

When I first became a principal, I worked at a small alternative high school for students who, for various reasons, could not or would not be a part of a traditional high school. The students were inspiring and fun to work with, but many had learning difficulties and behavioral issues that made working with them a daily challenge.

At that time, my small staff was primarily made up of young teachers who needed additional training and mentoring in methods of classroom management. Because their jobs were so demanding and exhausting, we often needed a substitute teacher. Licensed teachers on the substitute list were sometimes reluctant to come into our school because they were afraid of the tough population we served. But not Mr. F.

Although Mr. F. was a retired teacher and a man of advanced years, he was undaunted by our students, and he always answered our call for a substitute when we needed one. After several years of working with us, he chose to fill absences at our small school exclusively. I asked him one day why he was so willing to work with students who created so many challenges for teachers. His words floored me.

He told me that to teach troubled youth, one must first love kids – all kids, no matter their strengths or the problems they bring with them to school. He also explained that the harder it was to discover a student's gifts, the more rewarding the eventual payoff would be. My little school was my passion, and hearing that Mr. F. and I were kindred spirits in that regard warmed my heart.

Mr. F. firmly believed that troubled students benefit from every moment spent with a caring and skilled teacher. He knew that many of our students had significant behavioral and attendance problems, but he insisted they were still better off with every minute they spent in our school. Each student was a step closer to high school graduation, each student had an improved shot at a successful life, and each student was safe during the hours they spent with me and my staff.

I was stirred. Did he just say that every minute counts? He did, and he meant it. What an inspirational man! Mr. F. was comfortably retired. He had no need to be there for us. He had nothing except job satisfaction to gain from giving his time and talents to a little school that was trying to change the world, one troubled kid at a time.

Mr. F. was a gutsy guy. He did not look like a tough-minded teacher. He maintained high expectations in the classroom, but he was not a strict disciplinarian. Every member of our staff and every student in my small school loved him. He accepted the students exactly as they were while encouraging them to learn and achieve, and he had no doubt that our students and our staff members would succeed. Through one part-time position, Mr. F. managed to expand his social network with people of all ages and, by doing so, he changed the culture of our school for the better. I will be forever grateful to him.

Mr. F. lives in my memory as a role model. As I think about wisely using the remaining years of my life, I want to connect with other people like Mr. F. did. He used every opportunity to make a positive impact with every person he met. I thank Mr. F. for inspiring me to bring my A+ game every day. Because of him, I know that I can expand my network to include people I like, as well as people I can serve.

Mr. F., you were the best.

Networking journaling stem: Connection resources

Make a detailed and specific list of your current connection resources. Refer to the Connection Resources Record Sheet which can be downloaded from my website at www.reinventioninprogress.com/free -downloads.

EIGHT

Time: The Black Thread

We think about time in a variety of ways and, over the course of human history, we have become increasingly fixated on time. Although human beings are the only species known for keeping track of time in seconds, minutes, hours, days, months, years, decades and centuries, the passage of time affects all things. We humans are so focused on time, many of us spend our whole lives trying to accurately track its progress. We measure time with clocks, schedules and calendars. We set appointments and then obsess about arriving comfortably early or fashionably late.

Time seems to speed up when we are having fun and slow to an excruciating crawl when we are suffering; and, as we age, we begin to see that time is a limited resource. We all know, somewhere in the dark recesses of our minds, that one day our time on Earth will run out. There will be no more meetings to attend, no more appointments to keep, no more opportunities to do what needs to be done, feel what needs to be felt, say what needs to be said. We are all mortal, renting our bodies in which we house our souls, until the vessel into which we were born wears out.

When we are younger, we think we will live forever. Time is our friend and we often waste it as though our well of moments will never run dry. The passage of time will have no effect on us. Our generation will be immune from the winding down of the precious minutes of each day and night. We will always have our health, our energy, our lust for life.

Of course, this is folly, and I must admit that my generation became experts at putting off the ravages of time. We have perfected plastic surgery, hair implants and joint replacements to help us preserve the illusion that our time in the bodies we inhabit is limitless. We lift our faces, we lift our weights, we swallow our vitamins – all in an attempt to delay the inevitable.

In our linear understanding, time is fleeting and the tick tock of the hands on the clock will one day stop for all of us. But time existed before us and it will exist after we are gone. As we weave in the finishing threads of our reinvention process, how can we reconsider time as our ally instead of our enemy?

The little black dress

As we reinvent our lives in our fifties and beyond, we can embrace time in a new way. During the COVID-19 pandemic, many people of all ages began to reexamine their twentieth-century conception of the tyranny of time. Most of us have only a linear understanding of time, but in the world of physics time as it relates to space is far more complex. Although we are often ruled by deadlines and due dates, the universe is timeless. The color that immediately came to my mind as I considered the notion of universal timelessness was black.

Although in some cultures, black is regarded as the color of death, in the world of haute couture, black is the color of timeless sophistication and boldness. It conveys the style and competence of a person who has experienced much that life has to offer. There is a reason the "little black dress" is an elegant fashion statement that is reinvented with every generation. It makes a classic yet commanding statement about the growing power of the female experience that is possible today in many societies around the world.

As I considered the black threads of my new fabric, I realized I have owned a "little black dress" in every decade of my adult life. In my twenties, black made me feel sophisticated and hip. During my thirties, black helped me fit my feminine form into the serious world of work as it is frequently defined by men. In my forties, black was a power color. At fifty and beyond, I believed that black made me look thinner and more stylish. Thus, I adopted the "little black dress" that hangs in my closet today as my talisman for time.

Black is simplicity and complexity combined. The amalgamated colors in black reflect refinement and wisdom. Black incorporates a wealth of thought, moods, experiences, relationships, and the totality of my history, present moments, and all that is yet to come. Black is enduring and boundless. It carries the tone and tint of every skin color, every natural element, every particle of matter, every fiber of the universe.

Is time real?

The short answer to this question is, yes, at least in the way in which it is defined by many physicists practicing today. Time is real and has been studied by scientists and philosophers for centuries. While the exact nature of time is complex and is somewhat controversial among practitioners of variant disciplines, the fact is that in a very real sense, we all experience time every second we are alive.

As we have sought to make sense of our world, human beings have measured the passage of time with natural elements such as the daily 24-hour rotation of the Earth on its axis or the yearly revolution of the Earth around the Sun. We also use manmade clocks which are merely boxes containing mechanical works that repeatedly and predictably move at standardized rates. We can see natural and manmade movement, but we cannot see time.

While we cannot see time, we can see the consequences of its passage. In his 2010 book titled *From Eternity to Here: The quest for the ultimate theory of time*, physicist Sean Carroll explains that time " ...labels moments in the universe... measures the duration elapsed between events... " and "is a medium through which we move." With all that's been written about time, it's helpful to know that even though we can't see it, time is real and serves our need to make sense of how we fit into the world around us.

But time is not only studied in the field of science. Philosopher Henri Bergson's theory of real duration (1913) railed against mechanical and abstract scientific calculations about human experiences related to time and space. Bergson described duration as our "lived time," meaning how we experience the passage of time as compared to how we use human-made tools to mechanically measure time. In other words, we interpret time as we live our own experiences.

To illustrate, imagine you decide to make a cup of tea. You turn on the kettle to boil and you stand and watch as the heat of the burner transfers to the kettle and then to the water inside. Two long minutes go by, as indicated by the movement of the hands on your clock, yet your water is not yet boiling.

Frustrated, you turn your attention to something else. You pick up your tablet and reengage with a rousing game of online Scrabble. The friends you play with are formidable wordsmiths, and you quickly become absorbed with several games.

Suddenly, you hear the kettle whistling and your water is ready to make your tea. You glance at your clock and discover nine minutes have passed since you turned on the burner. You think, "That didn't feel like nine minutes. It felt like thirty seconds." Your choice to focus on something else while your water heated determined how fast time seemed to move, and your interpretation of your experience during that duration was that time "passed" less discernably when you were absorbed in action.

As we consider Bergson's idea about the perceived flexibility of duration, we can begin to see how our attitude toward time affects how we perceive our quality of life. Our age becomes less consequential. When our number of birthdays are ignored, our view of time is only impacted by our enthusiasm for living and the dynamism with which we approach affirming and energizing actions.

If we are content to see our days pass idly by, time may feel like it is slipping away, propelling us forward to our eventual demises. If, on the other hand, we think about how we want to use our remaining time on Earth to create a better future and fill our days with actions that are designed to help others, we can make time appear to slow down.

Life was meant to be lived as an experience, an unfolding story, minute by meaningful minute. In so doing, we will maximize our daily impact on those around us and attract people, places, and things that will make our later years the most joyful, powerful and loving of our lives.

Perception of time

The year 2020 was so packed with major life-changing moments, it often seemed we could not catch our collective breath. The world experienced massive fires in Australia, conflicts in the Middle East, a shake up in the British royal family, trade wars between the United States and China, a US presidential impeachment trial and election, drama around Brexit and the European Union, *Tiger King* on Netflix and massive dust clouds in the Sahara Desert.

COVID-19 spread globally, thrusting us into a collective state of anxiety about the health of our loved ones and ourselves. However, even as we struggled with the physical threat of the virus, we suddenly had to figure out how to live and work – at a distance. Many of us had to embrace Zoom and other meeting platforms to stay connected with family, friends and colleagues; people lost their jobs or had to work from home; kids couldn't go to school; we all stressed over getting enough toilet paper; people protested America's long history of systemic racism; masks became a political statement; the US president suggested injecting Lysol or drinking bleach; and we couldn't touch our faces, or date, or travel, or hug each other. Even though these events raced by and bombarded our senses every day in the news cycle, the months between February and December felt like ten years. Why?

Consider the perception of time. Children often perceive time as moving slower than adults. They experience much more novelty and process far more unknown mental images in a given day than an average grown-up. Thus, kids experience time as moving slower (Livni, 2019).

Conversely, the older we get, the fewer unusual sights and sounds we encounter. Adults spend less time than children highly engaged in making sense of the world in which they live. This was generally true, until the year 2020 when we were all required to deal with a constant onslaught of new information. When the human brain has lots to process, time seems to slow down (Livni, 2019).

Remember when you were a child and summer days seemed to stretch out endlessly before you? During my early summers, every morning my best friend and I asked each other, "What do you want to do today?" We rarely had a plan, so we killed at least an hour deciding how we should spend the glorious freedom of the day that rolled out like a red carpet before us. We exchanged ideas until one of us came up with a new game or an old activity that filled our coming hours with invention and action.

I recall that we were always on the move, always active, always busy – jumping headlong from one activity to the next. During those magical days, the passage of time seemed imperceptible. The same feeling occurs for anyone at any age who is engaged in a physical or mental activity that completely captures their interest. For many, by the time we reach the second half of our lives, every day feels like an unbridled race from morning until night. However, anyone can slow down the perception of time simply by packing more activity into each day (Livni, 2019).

What then can we conclude about our perception of time? We may have regrets about moments we wasted over the course of our lives. We may feel like we have missed our opportunity to travel the world, foster healthy relationships with our kids or find our one true love, but we can still attain these things in the second half of our lives. To do so, each of us is called to get up, get busy, and engage in activities that capture our imagination, keep our bodies moving, and slow down our perception of time.

Exercise, socialize, eat right, disconnect from unhealthy entanglements, serve others, share your resources, get involved and get excited about something. Take a stand and engage with life. Nothing slows down time like staying busy with something that ignites your passion. Embrace life and extend time!

Managing time intuitively

There are hundreds of resources you can use to manage your time and organize your life, your goals, your tasks, reminders of your tasks, and so on. Timers and schedules ensure that mundane errands get done, but as you reinvent your life, you can find greater freedom by relying more on your inner voice – your intuition – to determine how much time you spend on the missions that give your life meaning.

I devoted decades to demanding jobs that required me to account for every minute of my working day as well as many minutes of my time off. After I left the corporate world, I decided "No more." I began to listen to my heart and use my own intuition, my own inner voice to decide how to best fill my days with positive action.

This does not mean that I do not still use calendars and make appointments. I employ tools to help me manage my time, but they no longer dictate how long a call with a client will last or how long I will talk to a neighbor in my driveway. Clocks and calendars work for me to a point, but now they simply make sure I show up at an appointed time for a specific errand. Schedules no longer have the same power over me. Now I use my intuition to determine where I am needed most and for how long.

In years past, telling people at work that you were henceforth going to make your own schedule would have been blasphemous. In the twentieth and early-twenty-first century, corporations and businesses ran the show, but in this post-pandemic world, we have all learned how valuable our lives are. We know now how critical it is to spend quality *and* quantity time with our children and other family members. We have become acutely aware of how vital focused time and human touch are to our health and overall wellbeing.

It is now possible to complete jobs in flexible ways using online tools and social media. We can connect with people all over the world in ways that were not widely known prior to 2020. We can work in the morning, take the afternoon off, and work again for two or three hours in the evening. Night owls can work in the middle of the night. We can watch movies whenever we want and listen to music on demand. Therapy, medical advice, legal help, and food services are at our fingertips by using computers, smart phones and other devices.

COVID-19 devastated our society in myriad ways, but it forced us to slow down and take a break from the rapid pace of twenty-first-century life. We learned that there is indeed elasticity in how we use our own time. Today, time can be our friend no matter our age, so long as we understand that our choices can slow it down or speed it up. We can engineer time to suit our lives as we have never been able to do at this level before.

Time and our true purpose

When we resolve to live in closer alignment with our true purpose, we can begin to use time in accordance with our heart missions. After years of playing by other people's rules and ignoring the messages I received from my head, my heart, and my gut, I finally reached the point when I took control of time instead of allowing time to control me. Managing time with our intuition does not mean we abandon our common sense; it means that we exercise our in-born perception, subconscious awareness and sensory impressions when confronted by issues of time.

To use your intuition to determine how to spend your time, I suggest the following actions:

- **Get quiet:** Our intuitive selves usually speak to us in whispers to let us know when something is wrong or tell us the direction we should take. If we are to hear those soft voices, we must turn off our computers, silence our cell phones, take out our earbuds and spend quiet time mindfully listening.

- **Trust your gut:** As you are heeding messages from your gut, you must learn to trust what you hear. We often ignore these messages because we have no logical reason to accept their meaning. However, like many animals, we have perceptions that go far beyond what we see, hear, taste, smell and feel. Our inner selves are frequently true to their word.

- **Allow your autopilot to do its job:** Most autopilot systems function by knowing the standard operating procedures for completing a task. They automate steps so that sensors can detect needed actions without human awareness or intervention. We are each born with an autopilot system that takes over when the world around us becomes too scary or overwhelming. Your autopilot usually knows the next right thing to do. Learn to trust its advice.

- **Pay attention to your day and night dreams:** Our brains rest when we sleep and daydream, and our subconscious minds can help us access our intuition during these resting periods. By staying connected to our points of travel in waking and sleeping dreams, we can tell our conscious selves how to best use our time and give flight to our aspirations.

- **Engage in pencil play:** Writing and doodling can reveal things about us that only our intuition knows. I journal often and am usually surprised by what appears on the page. Some people use words for this process, and some prefer drawing or doodling shapes or pictures. Either way, your intuition will usually shine through in repeating words or phrases, patterns of thought or reiterative symbolism.

- **Break away from expectations and routines:** When life surprises us, we become more open to creativity and new possibilities. Try to solve a problem in a new way or alter your daily times for performing chores. By shifting your expectations of yourself and other people, you can see new ways to allow more freedom of thought and movement into your life. Skipping or changing a daily routine can reveal new ways to use your time to fulfill dreams and generate new possibilities. If you find yourself stuck in "That's the way I've always done it," it might be time for a change.

The timelessness of time

When we reach a certain age, it is easy to slide into the belief that time is no longer on our side. We become tempted by complacency and fear that we may have outlived our usefulness or relevance.

If we choose to redefine time, age becomes a nonissue and vitality becomes the focus. Time is a precious commodity, but it is not static. It can be stretched, elongated, and maneuvered so that we can engage in the work that is important to us during the second half of our lives.

I regard aging as a superpower. I have had my mettle tested and have somehow survived to this point. I have learned to enjoy each age along the way and fought off ageism and most other "isms" to fully accept myself as I am today. I have turned my back on despair and reached a magical time when I am now free to express my true feelings, to love to my heart's content, and to pass on my wisdom.

Time is no longer my enemy, but it does require my attention. I expect to remain vital, active and engaged with the business of living for the remainder of my time on Earth. To do less is to waste the precious gifts I receive daily. I choose to be creative with my time, to carefully decide how I spend it and with whom I share it. The people in my life deserve that, and so do I.

I have a lot more living to do before it comes time for me to surrender this life. As the Robert Frost poem goes, "…I have promises to keep, And miles to go before I sleep, And miles to go before I sleep" (Frost, 1923).

Time journaling stem:
Fill your days, slow down time

Think about how you spend your time every day. Record your activities in your journal for one week. Then, using your record as a guide, complete the How Do I Use My Time – Chart 1. Does Chart 1 reflect how you want to be using your time? If not, how might you alter your use of time to create a closer alignment between your reality and your dreams? Use Chart 2 to reallocate time to those things that feed your spirit and align with the reinvented dreams you hold for yourself. Both charts can be downloaded for free from my website at www.reinventioninprogress.com/free -downloads.

Conclusion:
What Will Your
Reinvented Life Look Like?

To weave a new piece of fabric, to change your life from gray to brilliant color, takes energy and thought, time and courage. It is not an instant process, but it does not have to take years. To reinvent yourself, you must be dedicated to your own wellbeing and aim to approach the second half of your life with a fresh outlook.

Now that you have bravely faced your past, processed your emotions and applied new information to the inconstancy of feelings, you are ready to reap the rewards. You have tools to nurture yourself, establish new values and envision what you want for yourself. An evolving support network and a revised perception of time will allow you to step into a reinvented future. What colors will your new fabric hold for you?

You have arrived at your New Beginning, but the details are yours to make real. A healing self-image and the excitement that comes with optimistic possibilities await. You have chosen your colors for a new piece of fabric – one that is not ripped or tattered or worn out. Your new fabric is strong and vibrant, and it will warm and protect you as you practice saying "yes" to novel experiences and relationships.

There are some who may find the thought of self-reinvention a childish fantasy. I respectfully suggest that these folks consider the lives of well-known women who followed their dreams and attained success during the second half of their lives:

- Laura Ingalls Wilder, writer of the *Little House on the Prairie* series of books, did not publish a word before age 65 (Trex, 2010).

- American painter Grandma Moses was a dedicated embroiderer before the pain of arthritis demanded she put down the needle and pick up a paint brush. She was 76 when she painted her first canvas, which she sold for $3. During the remaining 25 years of her life, she watched as her original paintings sold for $10,000 each (Trex, 2010).

- American actress Estelle Getty became "instantly" famous by playing Sophia Petrillo on a little show known as *The Golden Girls*. However, she had been a struggling actress for 40 years before securing her role at age 72 (Gaille, 2014).

- Ernestine Shepherd began to lift weights at age 56. At the time of this writing she is 84 and still works out regularly, but in 2010, she became the world's oldest female body builder (Prince, 2021).

- At age 70, Lisa Gable invented a bra strap that does not slip down over the shoulder. She went on to found and run a company called Strap-Mate (Lasseter, 1994).

- When Mary Tennyson was 63, her 92-year-old mother fell and broke her hip. Seeing her mom struggle with using a walker and managing a bag at the same time, Mary invented a purse that attaches to a walker: the StashAll (Horovitz, 2016).

I mention these fabulous women not because they are unusual, but because their experiences are becoming more common. They saw a need or developed an interest and refused to allow their number of birthdays to halt their quest for reinvention. For them, age was only a number on a calendar – and so it should be for all of us.

As for me, I will likely never retire. Over the course of my life, I have gone through multiple iterations of myself and I see no reason why the future should be any different. While my divorce was difficult, even excruciating at times, I am happy to report that I have stepped through the rip in my fabric and woven a new garment for myself that I intend to wear and alter for many years to come. I am now a published author, a self-supporting independent adult and a reinvented woman. None of us know how long we are going to live, but to stop reinventing before we reach the finish line is to stop living prematurely.

I have successfully regained color in my life, and you can too. I invite you to join me on this vibrant and exciting journey of reinvention. Just imagine how fabulous you will look in the colorful new garment you will piece together for yourself.

For more information regarding the process of reinvention, please visit my website at www .reinventioninprogress.com.

Bibliography

Al-Anon Family Groups, *How Al-Anon Works for Families & Friends of Alcoholics* (Al-Anon Family Group Headquarters, Inc., 2008)

Atwood, Ben, "5 ways Atheism can be spiritual" [blog post], thoughtcatalog.com (April 16, 2012), https://thoughtcatalog.com/ben-atwood/2012/04/5-ways-atheism-can-be-spiritual/

Bergson, Henri, *Time and Free Will: An essay on the immediate data of consciousness* (Dover Publications, 3rd ed., 2001, translated by F.L. Pogson)

Bradshaw, John, *Healing the Shame that Binds You* (Health Communications, Inc., 1988; rev. ed., 2005)

Bridges, William, *Managing Transitions: Making the most of change* (Da Capo Press, 1991)

Carroll, Sean, *From Eternity to Here: The quest for the ultimate theory of time* (Dutton, 2010)

Cherry, Kendra, "Locus of Control and your life" [blog post], verywellmind.com (December 7, 2019), www.verywellmind.com/what-is-locus-of-control -2795434

Cipoletti, Joy, "I stayed in my marriage too long – but I don't regret it" [blog post], divorcedmoms.com (June 1, 2014), https://divorcedmoms.com/i-stayed-in -my-marriage-too-long-but-i-dont-regret-it/

Delinsky, Barbara, *Escape* (Doubleday, 2011)

Dweck, Carol, *Mindset: Changing the way you think to fulfil your potential* (Little, Brown Book Group, 2012)

Ephron, Nora, *Heartburn* (Alfred A. Knopf, 1983)

Frankl, Viktor E., *Man's Search for Meaning: An Introduction to Logotherapy* (Beacon Press, 1962, Transl. Ilse Lasch)

Frost, Robert, "Stopping by Woods on a Snowy Evening", *New Hampshire* (Henry Holt, 1923)

Gaduoa, Susan Pease, "Are you among the grow- ing number of unhappy married people?" [blog post], *Psychology Today* (September 27, 2017), www .psychologytoday.com/us/blog/contemplating -divorce/201709/are-you-among-the-growing-number -unhappy-married-people

Gaille, Brandon, "10 people that found great success after turning 60" [blog post], *Brandon Gaille Small Business and Marketing Advice* (July 30, 2014), https://brandongaille.com/10-people-that-found-great-success-after-turning-60/

Greenspan, Miriam, *Healing Through the Dark Emotions: The wisdom of grief, fear, and despair* (Shambhala, 2003)

Harvard Medical School, "Understanding the Stress Response: Chronic activation of this survival mechanism impairs health," *Harvard Health Publishing* (July 6, 2020), www.health.harvard.edu/staying-healthy/understanding-the-stress-response

Horovitz, Bruce, "Getting rich after 50," *AARP Bulletin* (September 2016) www.aarp.org/work/working-after-retirement/info-2016/getting-rich-after-50.html

The Huffington Post Website, "Many unhappy in marriage but too scared to divorce, study finds" [blog post], *Huffington Post* (November 13, 2013), www.huffingtonpost.co.uk/2013/07/10/divorce-unhappy-marriage-secrets-_n_3572696.html?guccounter=1

Kelmenson, Kalia, "Building resilience in the body" [blog post], *Spirituality and Health* (February 6, 2020),

https://www.spiritualityhealth.com/blogs/the
-present-moment/2020/02/05/building-resilience-in
-the-body

Kessler, David, *Finding Meaning: The sixth stage of grief* (Scribner, 2019)

Kübler-Ross, Elisabeth, *On Death and Dying* (MacMillan Company, 1969)

Lansky, Amy, "The Community Guide: Identifying evidence-based approaches to achieve Healthy People 2030 objectives," (U.S. Department of Health and Human Services Office of Disease Prevention and Health Promotion, 2020) https:// health.gov/news/202010/community-guide-identifying-evidence-based-approaches-achieve-healthy-people-2030-objectives

Lasseter, Diana, "Entrepreneur solves problem of the slipping bra," The New York Times Online (December 11, 1994), www.nytimes.com/1994/12 /11/nyregion/entrepreneur-solves-problem-of-the -slipping-bra.html

Livni, Ephrat, "Physics explains why time passes faster as you age" [blog post], *Quartz* (January 8, 2019), https://qz.com/1516804/physics-explains-why -time-passes-faster-as-you-age/

Nall, Rachel, "Do amethysts have any proven healing properties?" [blog post], healthline.com (August 11, 2020), www.healthline.com/health/amethyst-healing -properties

Neuman, Fredric, "Why people in bad marriages stay married, or at least the reasons they give for staying married" [blog post], *Psychology Today* (July 13, 2014), www.psychologytoday.com/us/blog/fighting-fear /201407/why-people-in-bad-marriage-stay-married

Norwood, Robin, *Women Who Love Too Much: When you keep wishing and hoping he'll change* (Penguin Group, 1985)

Pillemer, Karl, *30 Lessons for Living: Tried and true advice from the wisest Americans* (Penguin Books Ltd., 2011)

Rogers, Everett, *Diffusion of Innovations*, 5th ed. (Simon & Schuster, 2008)

Prince, Diana, "Women's spotlight: The fit and fabulous Ernestine Shepherd, aging beautifully" [blog post], Birmingham Public Library Blog (April 20, 2021), https://bplolinenews.blogspot.com/2021/04 /womens-spotlight-fit-and-fabulous.html

Sanders, Robert, "Researchers find out why some stress is good for you" [blog post], *Berkeley News* (April 16, 2013), https://news.berkeley.edu/2013/04

/16/researchers-find-out-why-some-stress-is-good-for
-you/

Scott, Elizabeth, "Why emotional resilience is a trait
you can develop" [blog post], verywellmind.com
(April 28, 2020), www.verywellmind.com/emotional
-resilience-is-a-trait-you-can-develop-3145235

Seligman, Martin and Maier, Steve, "Failure to
escape traumatic shock," *Journal of Experimental
Psychology*, 74/1 (May 1967), 1–9

Selye, Hans, "The Stress Concept: Past, present and
future," in Cooper, C.L. (Ed.), *Stress Research: Issues
for the Eighties* (John Wiley & Sons, 1983), 1–20, www
.scirp.org/(S(i43dyn45teexjx455qlt3d2q))/reference
/ReferencesPapers.aspx?ReferenceID=1827323

Steinberg, Gregg, "Fall up and turn your tragedy
into transcendence," TEDx Talk, Rush U (August
12, 2015), www.youtube.com/results?search_query=
gregg+steinberg+ted+talk

Stepler, Renee, "Led by Baby Boomers, divorce rates
climb for America's 50+ population," Pew Research
Center (March 9, 2017), www.pewresearch.org/fact
-tank/2017/03/09/led-by-baby-boomers-divorce-rates
-climb-for-americas-50-population

Teresa, Mother, *A Simple Path* (Ballantine Hardcover,
1995)

Trex, Ethan, "Famous folks launched careers after 50" [blog post], *Mental Floss CNN* (May 16, 2010), www .cnn.com/2010/LIVING/worklife/05/16/mf.famous .career.after.50/index.html

Walker, Pete, *Complex PTSD: From Surviving to Thriving* (Azure Coyote, 2014)

Wheatley, Margaret J. and Frieze, Deborah, *Walk Out Walk On: A learning journey into communities daring to live the future now* (Berrett-Koehler Publishers, Inc., 2011)

Acknowledgments

As I have worked on this book, I have learned that writing is not the solitary experience I once imagined it to be. Like most things in life, it takes a village to create a book, and this one is no exception. When I began, I sought out the people and events that would facilitate my writing process – and, fantastically, the universe did not let me down. Therefore, I have many people to thank for their knowledge, patience, encouragement and love.

First, I want to thank my parents, LeRoy and Anita, who were my first teachers and who, for better or worse, empowered me to endure tough times, find a way forward and eventually solve my own problems. I also want to thank my sister, Terri, who taught me the true meaning of fortitude and courage. She was my first best friend, and thankfully, she is still a key player in my social network.

My sons, Greg and Chris, have been sources of unending strength and inspiration to me throughout my adult life. They have been beacons of love, joy, and motivation. They have pushed me forward, even when I wasn't sure I could take another step. They always believed in my ability to finish and publish this book and they gave me the courage to believe in myself. Thank you, gentlemen.

I have had many moments of joy, grace, hardship, failure, and victory over the years, and I would not have made it through without the love and encouragement of many family members and friends. I want to offer a special thank you to Stephanie P., Anne R., Larry and Terri Whitlock, Madeline Franco, Sharon Whitlock, Charlie and Roberta Whitlock, Mary Lynn Francis Chenoweth, Tina Dorsey, Shawn Coble and Amy Raymer.

A special thank you goes out to all those who urged me to write this book and heartened me to keep going, even when the going got tough. They include Grace Chatting, Lucy McCarraher, Joe Gregory, Kate Latham, Anke Ueberberg, Maya Berger, Jean Wolfe, Sue Williams, Stephanie Taylor, John Adams, Melanie Gow, Teresa Fitzsimmons, Kimberly Evans, Jeffrey Neubauer, Mark Morgan and Drew Lewellyn.

ACKNOWLEDGMENTS

Lastly, I want to thank my furry best friend, stress-reliever, playmate, snuggler-in-chief and writing partner, Matilda Whitlock. I could not have written this book without your faithfulness and constant companionship.

The Author

Cyndy Whitlock holds degrees in History, Secondary Education, and Special Education and is a licensed leader in academic and vocational education. She is perhaps best known as the founder and CEO of EduMagine, LLC, a company dedicated to helping individuals and organizations to promote leadership skills and successfully navigate change.

Over her 40-year career, she has been a teacher, principal, writer, speaker, and coach and has improved learning and personal achievement outcomes for many in the private and public sectors. Over the past ten years, she has expanded her focus to include helping herself and others to reclaim their power and achieve personal reinvention.

For more information about reinventing yourself, please visit my website, www.reinventioninprogress .com. There, you will find blog posts, free downloads to support your own reinvention process, reader testimonials and the personal stories of other women who have successfully stepped through the rips in their own fabric into lives of strength, self-love and personal reinvention.

🌐 www.reinventioninprogress.com
🔗 www.linkedin.com/in/cynthia-whitlock-0bb28237
📘 Edumagine Presents - Reinvention in Progress
📺 Reinvention with Cyndy Whitlock

You can also keep up with what my co-author, Matilda Whitlock, is doing at:

📷 www.instagram.com/meditationswithmatilda

Made in the USA
Las Vegas, NV
23 September 2021